Human Performance Models Revealed in the Global Context

A volume in
Adult Education Special Topics: Theory, Research and Practice in Lifelong Learning
Kathleen P. King, *Series Editor*

Human Performance Models Revealed in the Global Context

Edited by

Victor C. X. Wang
California State University, Long Beach

Kathleen P. King
Fordham University

INFORMATION AGE PUBLISHING, INC.
Charlotte, NC • www.infoagepub.com

Library of Congress Cataloging-in-Publication Data

Human performance models revealed in the global context / edited by Victor C.X. Wang, Kathleen P. King.

    p. cm. – (Adult education special topics)
  Includes bibliographical references and index.
  ISBN 978-1-60752-010-8 (pbk.) – ISBN 978-1-60752-011-5 (hardcover) 1. Human capital–Management. 2. Performance–Management. 3. Organizational learning. 4. Continuing education. I. Wang, Victor C. X. II. King, Kathleen P., 1958-
  HD4904.7.H8594 2009
  658.3'12–dc22

2008042372

Printed in the United States of America

CONTENTS

PREFACE

Victor C. X. Wang

Scholars (Rothwell & Dubois, 1998; Rothwell, Hohne, & King, 2007) define human performance as the end results or accomplishments desired from purposeful behavior or activity. Today's dynamic organizations are constantly seeking ways to achieve the end results or accomplishments desired from purposeful behavior or activity in order to stay ahead of the curve of developing and managing human capital. Matching the right solution or solutions to the right problem or problems, or using the right approaches to unleash human performance requires applying many different theories in practice. From andragogy to transformative learning, multiple intelligence to emotional intelligence, these learning theories and more are geared toward boosting human performance in a given organization, country, region or even a continent. Unless these theories are effectively applied to solving human performance problems or seizing human performance improvement opportunities, they will remain stale (King in Catapano, 2006). To build intellectual capital, establish and maintain a high-performance workplace, enhance profitability, and encourage productivity, requires human resource development (HRD) professionals, managers, researchers, practitioners, and employees to effectively apply learning theories in practice so that optimal training solutions may result in desired human performance.

Training is commonly understood as a necessary and important means to improving human performance. Gilley, Eggland and Gilley (2002) view training (HRD) as an important strategic approach to improved productivity, efficiency, and profitability. Swanson and Holton III (2001, p. 90) define training (HRD) as a process of developing and unleashing human expertise through organization development (OD) and personnel training and development (T&D) for the purpose of improving performance. Naturally, a book on human performance would be considered incomplete without addressing what learning theories lead to better training solutions. While traditional books may address needs assessment, designing training programs, transfer of training, and learning organizations, this book is designed to focus on critical issues of applying learning theories, workplace learning, human performance and training. Volume I of the book begins with an overview of many different learning theories involved in unleashing human performance in the workplace. Human performance is extensively critiqued and analyzed in light of how learning theories can be applied to lead to desired human performance. Readers of the book will benefit from the experiences and perspectives with our front line professors/scholars who have been developing and expanding important learning theories in the field.

As globalization brings different cultures together, human performance interventions and training solutions may be strained by cultures, policies and other lines of thinking specific to a particular country, region or continent. What is considered a systematic process of discovering and analyzing important human performance gaps, designing and developing cost-effective and ethically justifiable strategies to close those gaps, implementing the strategies, and evaluating the financial results in one country may not apply in another. For example, the well-reasoned theory of andragogy may be strained in an authoritarian country such as China where conforming to higher authorities is so valued. Is this situation true with Europe, Africa, South America or India?

As all sorts of human performance problems exist in today's organizations, dynamic organizations are not operated in isolation. Especially because organizations seek to build intellectual capital, establish and maintain a high-performance workplace, enhance profitability, and encourage productivity in a competitive relationship with other organizations world wide. Therefore, HRD professionals, managers, researchers, practitioners and employees need to develop a global perspective of effectively addressing human performance and training issues. Furthermore, the critical role of HR and training research has remained in today's global culture and marketplace as timely trend and undertaking worthy of investment.

Written by a group of highly respected authors in the field, Volume II of this book will reveal how to critically view human performance and training issues germane to a specific country, region or continent. Above all, readers are required to make connections between human performance and training issues in their own organizations and those in other places. Together, Volume I and Volume II of the book equip readers with knowledge, skills and attitudes to discover and analyze performance gaps, plan for future improvements in human performance, and design and develop cost-effective interventions to close performance gaps by applying appropriate learning theories and training solutions in today's dynamic organizations. *Human Performance and Training Issues* was developed to help researchers and practitioners select measures to be used in the evaluation of human performance and helps them seek better, more efficient and effective ways to close performance gaps in this global economy. The book is bursting with innovative ideas that will help readers create powerful solutions in their organization, their country, their region and their continent.

TARGET AUDIENCE

Human Performance and Training Issues should be of value to anyone interested in matching the right solutions to the right problems, addressing causes by providing a range of solutions to improve human performance in any organizations in the global economy. To build intellectual capital, establish and maintain a high-performance workplace, enhance profitability, and encourage productivity requires practitioners to go beyond a competency-based approach to training. From the theory of andragogy to the real cases provided by our highly respected authors, human capital developers and managers will be equipped with knowledge and skills to identify, solve and anticipate human performance problems in their respective organizations. Non-managers will also benefit from the book through identifying and solving day to day human performance problems because these problems are applicable to their work. Finally, for researchers, administrators and students who are looking forward to improving their research skills, our authors provide exemplary scholarly work in terms of how to conduct meaningful research in the area of human performance and training. Also, such a volume rich in identifying and seizing human performance improvement opportunities will help prepare our students to enter the real world of work.

ACKNOWLEDGMENTS

Any edited volume of work demands help and support from many people and this book is no exception. Allow us first to express our appreciation to our first rate authors for their time, patience and effort in preparing the much needed chapters for this book. Many of our authors are already tenured professors in the field. However, they all demonstrated a willingness to help with this volume and that truly required dedication to the profession that is beyond the norm.

Second, I wish to thank our editor/author, Dr. Kathleen P. King who has been a highly respected journal editor. She has been working with me on journal articles, book chapters and books all these years. Her insights have always been helpful in securing successful publications of my own scholarly work. Third, we want to express our appreciation to George Johnson whose editorial team has provided exceptional editorial work for our books. His innovations in publishing have benefitted researchers and academics worldwide. Fourth, we also appreciate the work of James J. King in copyedit and research support during the final manuscript preparation; he made the final stages of this large project much easier with his keen eye and patience. Finally, we thank our undergraduate and graduate students who have been patiently awaiting the publication of this book.

Victor C. X. Wang, Ed.D
California State University, Long Beach
Long Beach, CA

REFERENCES

Catapano, P. (2006, September 11). Interview with Kathleen P. King: Transforming education educators, and students with technology. *Inside Fordham Online.* Retrieved May 17, 2008, from: http://www.fordham.edu/campus_resources/ public_affairs/inside_fordham/september_112006/in_focus_faculty_and/ transforming_educati_23797.asp

Gilley, J. W., Eggland, S. A., & Gilley, A. M. (2002). *Principles of human resource development* (2nd ed.). New York: Da Capo Press.

Rothwell, W., & Dubois, D. D. (1998). Thoughts on human performance improvement. In W. Rothwell & D. D. Dubois (Eds.), *In action: Improving performance in organizations* (pp. 1–14). Alexandria, VA: American Society for Training and Development.

Rothwell, W., Hohne, C. K., & King, S. B. (2007). *Human performance improvement: Building practitioner competence.* New York: Elsevier.

Swanson, R. A., & Holton, E. F. (2001). *Foundations of human resource development.* San Francisco: Berrett-Koehler Publishers.

INTRODUCTION

Contextualization, the Marketplace, Meeting Room, Mao and More: The Global Context of Human Performance

Kathleen P. King

CULTURE AND CONTEXT

Scene I

> In a northeast corner of New England, in the United States, I was raised in the midst of towns named Apponaug, Pawtucket, Wampanoag, Narragansett and Montauk. What may have seemed strange words and sounds to others, were my neighboring communities. It was not until I was school age that I began to understand that these were Native American words and in many cases, tribal names.

Fast forward to today and we realize the depth and breadth of cultural roots not only extend to ourselves and our communities, but in bright variation across the world. With the ease and vividness of technology we can see, listen and experience cultures from today and yesteryear in increasing depth.

Human Performance Models Revealed in the Global Context, pages xi–xxii
Copyright © 2009 by Information Age Publishing

Indeed, part of this phenomenon has been popularly referred to by the author of *The World is Flat* (Friedman, 2006). However, I would maintain that globalization provides a rich opportunity to not only bridge the world in homogeneity, but also to celebrate the rich spectrum of multicolored hues.

Scene 2

We were overlooking the red sand hills and cliffs, watching the sun begin to set as the young boys played on the rocks and did not want to get back in the car.

Suddenly we heard a thundering pounding noise.

We soon realized the sound was not as close as we first thought.

In fact, it seemed to be coming from down the hill, but it sounded so close and now, it seemed; yes it was rhythmical.

They were drums playing; was there also chanting?

No, we could not make that out, but decidedly it was drumming.

We rode down to the display area and sure enough colorfully dressed Ute Native American Indians were drumming and dancing for the visitors. We were near the red rocks of the Gardens of the Gods in Colorado (n.d.) and the vision of human display, athleticism, grace, acrobatic movements, rhythm and music making seemed embedded in the landscape of the red caves, rocks, cactus and tumbleweed. Humanity and nature—color and movement—a lasting impression of indigenous human art as it was meant to be—in nature.

Rather than only looking through the colors of our own national flag, we have the opportunity to look at life through the perspective of our world neighbors. Consider the proximity we felt to different nations and cultures through:

- The devastation of a Chinese earthquake (Vause & FlorCruz, 2008), and 2004 Southeast Asian Tsunamis (National Geographic News, 2008),
- The struggles in Darfur since 2003 (Bloomfield, 2007) and War in Iraq (National Public Radio, 2008), and
- The triumphs of the 1983 fall of the Berlin Wall (CNN.com International, 2005).

Longstanding international events such as the Olympics help to celebrate our diverse heritage, roots and culture across generations and the world. However, even in the midst of the global reach of ubiquitous mass media, human nature is to be ethnocentric and self-centered.

Scene 3

The bright red, black and white, the tan of the wood and the shapes: bear, raven, whale and eagle, the art of the Pacific Northwest people from Native Americans to the First Nation of Canada depicts a life in nature and focus on simplicity that has always drawn me. I return again and again to this area. Across nearly thirty years of life it has already drawn me.

As much as I was raised in the blues and whites of the Iroquois people, it is this people group that draws me back. When I look at their work, I always see their stories, their understanding of the world. They made sense of the events around them, and they found meaning in their environment and determined to sustain themselves.

Indeed, Natives of the Pacific Northwest continue to be recognized and reckoned within their communities. Rather than overrun or cast out completely, they have mastered the land, and managed the invaders. What is it about these peaceful people who provide command of their situation over the centuries?

Deep roots between people and earth, world and history, we see it here.... Indigenous cultures remind us of these connections.

As we learn from the experiences, approaches, and strategies of other cultures, we cultivate opportunities for deeper understanding both individually and collectively. No group of people has all the solutions to business, training or human performance needs. Indeed, we are all colored and influenced by our own past and culture. From our studies we know our context, beliefs, assumptions, and values shadow, tint and flavor our ability to see and understand fully (King, 2005; Lussier, 2008).

Building upon this fact we can create greater richness! When we reach beyond our boundaries of nation, culture or discipline, we can also expand our realm of possibilities. Learning about experiences of human performance and training in cultures, settings, and circumstances different from our own, increases the opportunity for critical reflection, insight and innovation. The reason is because sometimes, as we see another's view, the flaws in our own views become more visible. Conversely, when I seek to communicate with those different from myself, I have to understand and address their context. Culture, practice, assumptions, values, and beliefs determine how they articulate with our expectations, and designs for training and assessment can "make or break" us.

Scene 4

I stared at the didgeridoo, boomerang and clackers: so different from what I had seen previously.

How frequently do these patterns of color occur?

What color are their mountains and desert sands?

What are their yearly seasons?

What are their worries?

What are their joys?

As I look at the objects and photos, I consider the Aboriginal people of Australia and wonder, how dissimilar or alike are we in our essential needs and being?

When we bring the message of training and learning to the context and culture of others, we accomplish contextualization. We have to be able to step outside of ourselves, take the view of the "Other" and enjoy the magnificence of humankind. There are great potential, energy and production when we accomplish this transformation of the message and the means. It takes human insight to make this leap; it takes human potential to translate it into human performance outcomes.

OVERVIEW

As we consider the needs of the field of human resources, the most prominent need, in terms of combined depth and breadth of potential, is training. In the business realm, one could rise to supremacy or fall to oblivion on the basis of spurious daily events. However, more frequently those individuals and organizations which strategize, plan, learn, proceed, and continually revaluate their plans, are the ones who will have the best chance at success.

The rich multiple contexts in which human resource development is manifested and understood around the worlds is a storehouse of wealth for trainers, mangers, employees, and organizations. Increasing our understanding of what and how other organizations and cultures approach the many dimensioned opportunities and challenges of human performance and training, can unleash new directions for all. Human potential and possibilities are unbounded; human resource development is the means to codify, accelerate, direct and provide the means to equip workers and their collective organizations to reach their desired goals (organizational development) (see Yorks, 2005).

Scanning this field with a theme of "The Marketplace, Meeting Room, Mao and More" provides an opportunity to focus on not only competition and fiscal outcomes, but also the workplace organization and climate, and the intersections of work and government, organizations and policy, change and status quo. The very powerhouse of human performance is of course the potential of humankind.

In this chapter, I will briefly present critical considerations of these themes to serve as an introduction to this volume. My intent is to provide a vision, stir your thoughts, and open your mind to the adventure these books, *Human Performance and Training Issues* (Wang & King, 2009a) and *Human Performance Models Revealed in the Global Contexts* (Wang & King, 2009b) may hold for you and your organization.

THE MARKETPLACE

Human resource is specifically identified as serving the needs of people and organizations in the workplace. More specifically the area of human performance and training addresses how preparing, guiding, supporting and improving the relevant knowledge base and work skills of employees will improve organizations (Banks, 2009; Bierma, 2009; Noe, Hollenbeck, Gerhart, & Wright, 2007).

Rather than mandatory formal education, workplace learning is situated in an environment of real world application. In addition such preparation is often provided at the time of needed implementation so that transfer of learning may occur immediately. By tightly coupling the learning experience with outcomes and action, urgency, relevance and need are often clearly evident to all participants (Caffarella, 2001).

The larger perspective of this dynamic is that people and organizations operate within a larger, dynamic exchange. Indeed whether an organization is commercial, government, nonprofit, or non-government organization (NGO) they transact business within a designated "marketplace."

In the broadest sense, this marketplace may be considered the exchange of goods and services. Therefore, it is achieved when the goods and service of one organization or individual are traded in cash or likeness for that of another.

Obviously when one works for an organization which is focused on local commerce or trade, local conditions will dominate the ebb and flow of conditions. However, all marketplaces are impacted nonetheless by global events and dynamics. The pervasiveness of worldwide media in a plethora of formats, inexpensive and rapidly progressing technology, and globalization, our individual and collective decisions have brought a significant change (Handwerk, 2005). These factors determine one's place in a global, rather than solely local, *marketplace* at every turn and much more quickly than a few years ago.

Indeed, the choices organizations make about training and performance will ultimately impact their production, viability and level of success. When organizational leadership perceives this vital connection, they place a strong emphasis on the related topics. The definitions, evaluation, support and progress of human performance in turn become critical benchmarks to boards of directors, executive leadership, management and staff (Caffarella, 2001).

Organizations which are led and managed well will have the ability to dynamically articulate and impact make strategic planning, production, employment and other fiscal agendas in concert with human performance and training. When leadership and staff of organizations realize the critical connections between "the bottom line" and human performance, they discover a vital link for directing, energizing and sustaining their impact. When theses elements become unlinked, or uncoupled, the articulation, and coordination, of the organization is in jeopardy (Scott, 1992).

MEETING ROOM

In our scan of organizational themes which emerge in these volumes, the meeting room is another significant element I have selected to highlight. To me the "meeting room" represents the broad scope of training itself. Sampling just a few dimensions of this broad topic, I suggest it includes, but is not limited to, foundations of training models, adult learning strategies, educational philosophies, job descriptions, assessment, performance reviews, outcomes, human relations, classroom management, program planning, instructional design, and distance learning.

In the world of work, the broad concept of training is much more than a mandated curriculum, seat time to win a diploma, or academic pursuits separated from application. Training has urgency, a critical opportunity for application which can be used to captivate, motivate, and improve skills and performance.

One of the frameworks that I frequently refer to as an essential prerequisite for success in training is the understanding of context, content and learners. These criteria emphasize that rather than the rote, disconnected reproduction of a cookbook of human recipes for learning effective training is dynamic, customizable and relevant. These volumes fully voice and demonstrate this orientation.

Unfortunately many people participating in professional learning in the workplace may not have experienced such training. This book's authors and editors have worked hard to develop individual chapters and a collective, which fill these gaps, flesh out the details, provide vision and strategies to change the world of training.

MAO

To introduce the next organizational themes which emerged in my thematic study of these volumes, I use "Mao" as a catchphrase, or representation. In this case "Mao" is that theme which characterizes the political or nationalistic influences impacting human performance and training.

Salient points to realize about these texts are that we have a plethora of international scholars participating in its development. We are fortunate to have many different sectors of business, but also a wide representation of political and national identities. To name several of the countries explicitly identified in this area, I draw your attention to China, India, Africa, the European Union, the United States, South America, Caribbean, Germany and more. In addition we see chapters which address situations under the rule of communism, collectivism, democracy, capitalism, cooperatives, fluctuating governmental regimes, monarchies, colonies, and parliaments.

Why do I draw attention to nations and politics when discussing learning in the work place? It is because we cannot separate learning from context. The historical, political and cultural contexts of people impact the learning opportunities available to workers. In addition it may also dictate the freedom, or not, to engage in change for individuals, groups or businesses. When governments dictate production criteria or rates, when regulations determine limits or tariffs on imports and exports and when educational philosophies are controlled or "guided" by national, cultural or religious politics and ideological preferences trainers, human resource specialists, and managers must cope with these issues explicitly.

For some people having to cope with issues of governmental control over training agendas or training purviews is unthinkable. For other groups, it is a way of daily life and survival or failure. Short of visiting all these many dimensions of variation firsthand, this book offers both insight, perspectives and in some cases, realistic case studies to develop our insight and practice further.I remember that when I was editing the book, *Comparative Adult Education around the Globe* (King & Wang, 2007), I was moved to tears when I read about adult learners in Egypt climbing in through windows before class in order to secure seats (Daffron & Riedel, 2007). And my amazement at the role craftsmanship supported by indigenous adult learning has impacted the gross national product (GNP) of Thailand (Strohschen, 2007).

In much the same way, although I have studied Soviet Union and China since I was a teenager, I was not prepared for the descriptions of real cases of human performance and training included in this text, for example, of Mao (Wang, 2009) and also the European Union in this volume (Strohschen, 2009). In the volume *Human Performance Models Revealed in the Global Context,* our authors and editors have selected vital cases to illustrate critical experiences and patterns influenced by a host of influences around the world. The result is that readers now have available to them a host of varied cases in this topic area for individual, group and small group study reflection, and practice.

In the *Fundamentals of Human Performance and Training* volume, readers will find a wide variety of critical topics, theories, perspectives and practices which we had found to be less accurately or less frequently addressed in the literature. In addition, you will find overviews and responses to current trends, past models and upcoming approaches in these chapters. When so many books today are barely sufficient to cover the basics of human performance topics, this pair of books provides a complementary group which we hope will be added to in the future with additional volumes and editions.

By digging into the past, and scanning current and future trends many times with nationals from the discipline and original setting, we have a unique opportunity. Readers will discover that the authors present, analyze, commentate and operationalize essential elements to drive organizational development and growth. Rather than relying on the "way we have always done it," these texts provide a storehouse of information and insight to revitalize and direct management and workers. One of the outstanding benefits of this collection is that no matter where you are in the production year or area of responsibility in an organization, you will find guidance. These texts offer rare, substantial and practical insight and resources for trainers and leaders around the world, specializing in many fields, governments, cultures, markets and models.

MORE

The theme of "More" within this introductory chapter title illustrates the fact that many other facets, influences, frameworks and perspectives of human performance and training are discussed in these books in depth. From socioeconomic conditions to globalization, different business sectors to adult learning, and diversity to technology, the strands of variation abound in this collective work.

Yet upon reading the chapters of the books, it is vividly revealed that these issues, trends, and influences variously impinge upon, direct, precipitate, obliterate, promote and dominate the agendas of human performance and training. It becomes all too evident that global trends can drive production, budgets and thereby supply and demand for workers in even seemingly isolated environments. At the same time, one might see the boom of industries that one might see in the same country a dearth of demand due to cost, restrictions or oversupply. In the 21st century, one cannot separate commerce and the training and cultivation of human potential from the technologies which make it more available.

During a time when teens and young adults use cell phones and text messaging like their elders used "snail mail" and corded telephones with dials and analog bells, industry and professional workplaces cannot continue to let the world of technology pass it by. Globalization is creating a terrific demand for information literacy and technology literacy skills among workers of most job descriptions (Egan, 2009; King & Sanquist, 2009). In addition, those employees who think critically, problem solve and collaborate will more likely succeed in the 21st century workplace than those who cannot. Another requisite training trend is to not over train people. This trend has emerged today because we see that usually adults have multiple different careers and may never use advance beyond basic protocols.

Differentiation, specificity and voice development are key elements we also see. Differentiation and specificity of training provide powerful "just in time" learning. While we also know cross training and collaboration develops efficiencies, communication, and depth of organizational mission and effectiveness (Bierma, 2009; Schmidt, Mott & Lanoux, 2009; Ziegler & Mottern, 2009). Additionally, when cultivated effectively issues of worker voice and potential provide tremendous opportunity to tap talent, motivation, creativity and direction for organization production, profits and leadership (Alfred, 2009; Banks, 2009; Beck, 2009).

CONCLUSION

As one considers the variety of manifestations of human performance in business and workplaces around the globe, one has to be amazed that there is a continuity of approaches evident. Additionally, these two volumes demonstrate that while there are similarities, common frameworks, ideologies and trends, there are also both complexity and ubiquity in this area. The patterns and divergences, seen in theory and practice of human performance and training across the world, provide the basis for this much needed, meaningful, and profound discussion. Furthermore, to our knowledge, these volumes' total contribution is unmatched in its global perspective, diverse breadth of expertise, and format. From research to case study, historical and political analysis to instructional design, (to name a few examples) these books provide a compelling portrayal of the global context, needs, and opportunities.

Included in the discussions are not only prominent, global and national issues, but also the trends which have emerged, their roots, history and results. In addition, our expert authors provide vibrant accounts of both the promise and realization of human performance for professional growth, corporation success, national advances and vigilant attention to policy.

I hope that as you embark on the journey of experiencing this book, you will take time now and periodically to reflect on that great potential with which we have been entrusted. As the sage says, "With great ability, comes great responsibly."

As professionals with a greater understanding of human performance and training around the globe you will gain insight into varied perspectives, practices and values. Through the cultivation and development of human beings, training and development, insightful and responsible management and leadership we can protect, design, direct, enlarge and innovate the future. Consider whether and how you will vitally participate with the book's authors and editors in being part of the answer to the need for shaping the future of human resources, human performance and training. We have so much more to discover, and so many more lives to improve!

REFERENCES

Alfred, M. (2009). Diversity, culture, and human performance in work organizations. In V. C. X. Wang, & K. P. King (Eds.), *Human performance and training issues.* Charlotte, NC: Information Age Publishing.

Banks, C. (2009). Critical human performance issues in the United States. In V. C. X. Wang, & K. P. King (Eds.), *Human performance models revealed in the global context.* Charlotte, NC: Information Age Publishing.

Beck, J. (2009). Examining human performance in South America. In V. C. X. Wang, & K. P. King (Eds.), *Human performance models revealed in the global context.* Charlotte, NC: Information Age Publishing.

Bierma, L. (2009). Human performance theory and practice: A review of its contributions and limitations. In V. C. X. Wang, & K. P. King (Eds.), *Human performance and training issues.* Charlotte, NC: Information Age Publishing.

Bloomfield, S. (2007, April 30). *Darfur: War without end.* Retrieved May 25, 2008 from, http://www.independent.co.uk/news/world/africa/darfur-war-without-end-446777.html

Caffarella, R. S. (2001). *Planning programs for adult learners: A practical guide for educators, trainers, and staff developers* (2nd ed.). San Francisco: Jossey Bass.

CNN.com International. (2005, May 31). *Fall of The Berlin Wall 'a defining moment.'* Retrieved May 25, 2008, from http://edition.cnn.com/2005/WORLD/europe/05/31/defining.moments.25/index.html

Daffron S. R., & Riedel, A. (2007). The challenges of educating adults of the Middle East and North Africa. In K. P. King, & V. C. X. Wang (Eds.), *Comparative adult education around the globe* (pp. 31–58). Hangzhou, PR China: Zhejiang University Press. Worldwide distribution: Transformation Education LLC. (www.transformationed.com)

Egan, T. M. (2009). Theories and practice on training in the global community. In V. C. X. Wang, & K. P. King (Eds.), *Human performance and training issues.* Charlotte, NC: Information Age Publishing.

Friedman, T. (2006). *The world is flat.* New York: Farrar, Straus and Giroux.

Garden of the Gods. (n.d.). *Park history.* Retrieved May 25, 2008, from http://www.gardenofgods.com/parkinfo/index_253.cfm

Handwerk, R. (2005, January 28). *Tsunami blogs help redefine relief effort.* Retrieved May 25, 2008, from: http://news.nationalgeographic.com/news/2005/01/0126_050126_tv_tsunami_blogs.html

King, K. P. (2005). *Bringing transformative learning to life.* Malabar, FL: Krieger.

King, K. P., & Sanquist, S. (2009). 21st century learning and human performance. In V. C. X. Wang, & K. P. King (Eds.), *Human performance and training issues.* Charlotte, NC: Information Age Publishing, Inc.

King, K. P., & Wang, V. C. X. (Eds.). (2007). *Comparative adult education around the globe.* Hangzhou, PR China: Zhejiang University Press. Worldwide distribution: Transformation Education LLC. (www.transformationed.com)

Lussier, R. (2008). *Human relations in organizations: Applications and skill building* (7th ed). New York: McGraw-Hill Higher Education.

National Geographic News. (2008, January 18). *Tsunami in Southeast Asia: Full coverage.* Retrieved May 25, 2008, from: http://news.nationalgeographic.com/news/2005/01/0107_050107_tsunami_index.html

National Public Radio (NPR). (2008). *The toll of the war: Interactive.* Retrieved May 25, 2008, from: http://www.npr.org/news/specials/tollofwar/tollofwarmain.html

Noe, R., Hollenbeck, J., Gerhart, B., & Wright, P. (2007). *Fundamentals of human resource management* (2nd ed.). New York: McGraw-Hill Higher Education.

Schmidt, S., Mott, V., & Lanoux, J. (2009). Using principles of adult learning to improve human performance. In V. C. X. Wang, & K. P. King (Eds.), *Human performance and training issues.* Charlotte, NC: Information Age Publishing.

Scott, W. R. (1992). *Organizations: Rational, natural and open systems* (3rd ed.). Upper Saddle River, NJ: Prentice Hall.

Strohschen, G. (2007). Adult education praxis in Thailand. In K. P. King, & V. C. X. Wang (Eds.), *Comparative adult education around the globe* (pp. 11–30). Hangzhou, PR China: Zhejiang University Press. Worldwide distribution: Transformation Education LLC. (www.transformationed.com)

Strohschen, G. (2009). Panorama for global education and training of adults: A kaleidoscopic view at the European Union experience. In V. C. X. Wang, & K. P. King (Eds.), *Human performance models revealed in the global context.* Charlotte, NC: Information Age Publishing, Inc.

Vause, J., & FlorCruz, J. (2008, May). *Nearly 10,000 reported killed in China quake.* Retrieved May 25, 2008 from: http://www.cnn.com/2008/WORLD/asiapcf/05/12/china.quake/

Wang, V. C. X. (2009). Human performance in China. In V. C. X. Wang, & K. P. King (Eds.), *Human performance models revealed in the global context.* Charlotte, NC: Information Age Publishing, Inc.

Wang, V. C. X., & King, K. P. (Eds.). (2009a). *Human performance and training issues.* Charlotte, NC: Information Age Publishing.

Wang, V. C. X., & King, K. P. (Eds.). (2009b). *Human performance models revealed in the global contexts.* Charlotte, NC: Information Age Publishing.

Yorks, L. (2005). *Strategic human resource development.* Mason, OH: Thomson-Southwestern.

Ziegler, M., & Mottern, R. (2009). Informal learning and performance. In V. C. X. Wang, & K. P. King (Eds.), *Human performance and training issues.* Charlotte, NC: Information Age Publishing.

CHAPTER 1

MOVEMENT TOWARD STAYING AHEAD OF THE CURVE IN DEVELOPING AND MANAGING HUMAN CAPITAL

John A. Henschke

INTRODUCTION

Developing and Managing Human Capital in corporations have required extensive monetary investment for years. This has been necessary for workers to keep abreast of changes that continue to take place in the Human Capital Management Field in the way products are made and distributed, and services are provided throughout the world. Thus, the idea that continuing learning as a lifelong process has gained momentum as the pace of Human Capital Development and Management accelerates.

To address this need, corporations have established Training Departments (TD) to provide technical information and knowledge for the development and management of human capital. Generally the trainers (human capital developers and managers) in each technical area have operated

Human Performance Models Revealed in the Global Context, pages 1–27
1

quite separately from trainers in other technical areas, and have not functioned cooperatively for the corporation's benefit. This takes workers from their work setting and into a center for a period of time, where trainers provide them with the current human capital technical information in a particular area; then they return to their work setting. Moreover, this has resulted in those corporations falling behind the 'curve' in human capital development and management.

Watkins and Marsick (1993) warn that the connection between leveraging human capital, learning, and organizational survival seems to be emerging as inseparable. Organizations realize that they will not survive if they do not change in the ways required to leverage human capital. The result of this need to change is a push toward continuous learning for continuous improvement. Some of the influences moving organizations in the direction of staying ahead of the curve in human capital management include: Changes in technology that require learning; a service orientation that calls for learning; high-performing and self-directing teams that necessitate learning; participatory management which entails learning; time savings that entail reducing learning cycle time; and, global turmoil and competition that require continuous information as changes occur overnight.

Armed with this awareness, some companies are taking action by engaging personnel in their training department with a learning process to update their learning abilities, and implementing a more humane work process. Beyond that some are seeking to align the TD with Adult Educators within Universities, and are calling on that expertise to help them move the TD toward becoming a 'Performance Support Department' (PSD). This means that these adult educators engage the TD as a community of learning and practice in becoming a 'cutting-edge change team' to manage human capital more effectively and support the performance of the workers in the corporation.

The author has had some experience as an adult educator in the process described above, on reorienting a corporate training department toward supporting workplace and performance in human capital development and management, with various organizations/corporations. He has gained some insights about what has worked thus far in that situation and some things that need to be considered or included in 'staying ahead of the curve in developing and managing human capital'. Following are some of the recent research and practice ideas surrounding this topic of helping participants stay ahead of the curve in human capital management: Shifting from 'training' to 'performance support' while in the work setting; managing, leveraging, and implementing the total system of its own human capital resources to transform itself into a cooperating and flourishing entity for accomplishing the corporate mission; and, applying what is known to what is done with the various constituencies they serve.

This chapter is organized around various themes that have emerged in the process: Elements in Preparing and Planning for Change in Developing and Managing Human Capital; Required Competencies of the Change Agent in Developing and Managing Human Capital; Methods for Implementing Change/Making Change Happen in Developing and Managing Human Capital; and, Organizational Goals and Results from Changing in Developing and Managing Human Capital.

ELEMENTS IN PREPARING AND PLANNING FOR CHANGE IN DEVELOPING AND MANAGING HUMAN CAPITAL

Knowles (1986, 1989) suggests that there are three basic strategies for introducing change into a system or organization. Edict—successful only if we have the authority to enforce change and those who are going to have to implement it are adequately prepared. Persuasion—successful only if we are in a position in which people will listen to us, and we are persuasive. Piloting and osmosis—successful only if we release everyone to be responsible and in charge of their own learning and their own projects. Probably most changes involved with helping a Training Department in a corporation transform itself into a Performance Support Department, would entail parts of all three strategies.

Kirkpatrick (1985) asserts a need for awareness by those initiating change, of two different responses to change, resistance and/or welcoming. On the resistance side of change, people may perceive it as: meaning personal loss (security, money, pride and satisfaction in work, etc.); not needed; doing more harm than good; being proposed by those who lack their respect; being made in an objectionable manner; arousing their negative attitude toward the company; a personal criticism; creating burdens; requiring effort; having bad timing; a challenge to their authority; and/or, only second hand information they received. On the welcoming side of change, some may perceive it as: personal enhancement (security, money, authority, responsibility, status/privilege, self-satisfaction); taking less time and effort; providing a new challenge; being proposed by those they respect; reducing boredom; providing opportunity for their input; supporting their desire for change; being timed right; and/or, presented in a manner to their liking.

Kirkpatrick also proposes benefit from a number of possible areas of questions to be asked prior to considering organizational change in human capital management. How will those involved react? How will the change get accepted? How rapidly should this change be implemented? How will these changes affect other departments? What if someone asks for a change others consider a mistake? Should the 'boss' be made aware of a proposed change before one decides to move ahead? What if a change does not work out? Should all levels of personnel be involved in deciding and implementing change? How far ahead in time should change be communicated?

To make certain we lay the groundwork for success in developing and managing human capital, Hackman (2004) identifies five essential conditions that greatly enhance the likelihood of a human capital team success. They are: a stable team, a clear and engaging direction, an enabling team structure, a supportive organizational context, and the availability of competent coaching.

Caroselli (2001) cautions that your client's strategic plans are worthless if they are written without a strategic vision in mind. Failing to be 'externally aware' can result in incomplete plans. And failing to articulate a vision can create a hole in the fabric of those plans. The following five steps afford an opportunity to marshal the strengths of the present in order to diminish the impact of weaknesses in the future: Begin by asking the right questions; determine the external events impacting the vision; taking care not to be overly influenced by what could be characterized as the brilliance of transient events; state the vision; develop plans based on that vision; and, implement the plan, communicating it as often as possible.

Myrna (2007) provides a comprehensive conceptual framework that unifies strategic planning for development and management of human capital concepts into a simple and seamless flow between the foundation and accompanying tactics. Vision is the foundation which is stable from five to 30 years. The next level is the mission that is stable for three to five years. Then comes strategy with its stability for one and a half to three years. Next on the pyramid are the goals that are in place for one year, to one and a half years. Results are expected to be stable for 12 months. Actions are based on a 90-day cycle. The pyramid holds together cohesively in that today's actions lead to fulfilling the vision, and it is the vision that drives today's actions.

Simmerman (2001) proposes that discussion of organizational change be conducted with personnel in the corporation in such a way that it will: generate a high level of creativity and discovery and capture the benefits of diversity of thinking and perspective; generate a high degree of interactivity and action learning; confirm that current systems and processes are generally less than optimal; stimulate a discussion on change or continuous quality improvement; identify new ideas and solutions to solve difficult problems; focus on learning organization approaches and change the language of organizational improvement—a powerful approach to change management; and, challenge existing beliefs about how the organization really works.

Taylor et al. (2000) remind us that when we talk about change, typically we have focused our idea of change exclusively on a change in behavior, even in learning. However, they insist that we must undergo a very fundamental change (and transformation) in how we think about change. It is that we need, possibly would be well advised, no, we must know how we think we know what we think we know. And this change is not in behavior, it is a change in our epistemology—our way of knowing, or the theory that investigates the basis of our knowledge. We must have some understanding of the epistemology of change as we prepare and plan for change. If we do not, we will be hard pressed, if not totally unprepared to respond to those adult learners who want an answer that makes sense to them as to why they should learn something—or change—before they are willing to consider whether or not they will 'sign on' to any change that is proposed.

Just as there is a required environment/climate (soil, water, sunshine, elimination of weeds, cultivation, time, food/fertilizer) that is conducive for plants to grow, so there is also an environment/climate necessary that is conducive for human beings to mature as they are involved in learning and changing to stay ahead of the curve in human capital management. Bennett (1961) advances the thought that the most important task of those leading change is creating a climate that is conducive to the change being attempted. This is something other than rational—it is an emotional atmosphere (environment/climate) in which people feel that those leading in change are empathic and nonjudgmental toward them and their needs. This is a climate in which persons will be more open about their feelings and resistance. And it is important for those leading change to understand this beforehand, so that they will plan and prepare to make provision for this climate conducive to learning in the change process.

Schneider (2001) asserts that adaptability rather than speed or strength, is the crucial requirement for survival amidst navigating the sea of change. Participants are helped to identify how they can help themselves and their organizations achieve a more positive change climate.

Additionally, Bennett (1961), anticipating some of what emotional intelligence quotient (EIQ) researchers would claim nearly 40 years later (Goleman, 1998; Sterrett, 2000; Warner, 2001), goes on to say that in any planned change those leading must give as much attention to the emotional dimension as is given to the informational aspects of the change effort. People are somehow not persuaded out of their resistance and objections. However, they can be released from their fears when they are adequately informed and their feelings may be openly expressed and accepted. Goleman, Sterrett and Warner indicate that based on a number of recent studies, Intelligence Quotient (IQ) or general intelligence appears to contribute no more than 25% to one's overall success, with strong technical competence or specific intelligence in one's chosen field contributing 10–20% to one's success equation. They suggest that the remaining 55–65% of one's level of success formula comes from their ranking on the dimensions of Emotional Intelligence.

Sterrett (2000) defines true emotional intelligence as being able to appropriately call upon information from the emotional center of one's brain, and balance that information with the rational center of one's brain. Goleman (1998) indicates that emotional competence is made up of five dimensions: Empathy—awareness of others' feelings, needs, and concerns; social skills—adeptness at inducing desirable responses in others; self-awareness—knowing one's internal states, preferences, resources, and intuitions; self-regulation—managing one's internal states, impulses, and resources; and, motivation—emotional tendencies that guide or facilitate reaching goals.

Carrol (2001) gives a clear picture about how to initiate and manage change. Today's combination of external and internal workplace pressure guarantees that every organization must face change. Because change represents some elements of the unknown, it implies risk. The organization undergoing change can risk its human, physical, and technological resources, its collective knowledge, even its competitive marketplace position in attempting to handle change. Risk demands that organizations plan for change, rather than waiting for it to happen and then trying to cope after the fact. The seven steps in the planned change process are: Establishing your mission and purpose; auditing your current organization; scanning your external environment; conducting market research; creating a continuum—short-term and long-term goals; developing and implementing an action plan; and, integrating change planning into your system.

Wagner (2001) reminds us that unless facilitated properly, otherwise effective presentations and change in developing and managing human capital can be derailed by audience resistance, even management. Personal agendas, difference in values and interpersonal styles, and competition for organizational resources can all contribute to resistance in group settings. As a way to learn to deal with resistance, one may simulate a meeting with members of the audience: Presenter (VP Human Resources); Plant Manager; First-Shift Supervisor, Union Representative; General Manager; Vice-President of Finance and Operations; and, Vice-President of Marketing and Sales. Structure the meeting to record procedures for each participant and their answers to the following questions: (1) What did he or she say and do? (2) How did the VP of Human Resources respond? (3) How effective was the response? (4) Suggestions for improvement.

Vega (2001) focuses on strategic planning of change, providing a situational analysis in four areas of business: Strengths, weaknesses, opportunities, and threats. Strengths and weaknesses cover internal issues, and opportunities and threats are external or environmental issues. Effective strategic planning requires a careful analysis of all four areas.

However, we must remember that even strategic planning is changing. Devane (2001) argues that the nature of strategic planning has changed dramatically in the past few years. These changes have been in response to the increasingly difficult environment in which corporations must operate: global markets, unexpected new competitors, and dizzying technology changes. All these factors create an environment in which it is difficult to develop any sort of continually relevant, long-term plans that have lasting significance.

These factors may provide insights into how well an organization's strategic plan positions organization for success in today's turbulent business environment. But searching for more detail may be helped by the categories for changes including: Strategic focus, organizational identity, environmental scans and plans, internal scans and plans, products and services, reinvention and renewal, performance measurement, leadership, and strategy process effectiveness.

REQUIRED COMPETENCIES OF THE CHANGE AGENT IN DEVELOPING AND MANAGING HUMAN CAPITAL

The first year this author worked with the Training Division of a major corporation, in leveraging their transformation into a Performance Support Division for getting and staying ahead of the curve in developing and managing human capital, was devoted to developing a list of competencies required. These included emotional intelligence, for them to carry on the work of Adult Educators/Human Resource Developers. This included three roles (Instructor, Supervisor, and Futurist), fourteen sub-roles, with a total of 200 competencies. In all the array of competencies, one of the sub-roles that they need to be able to perform is that of a Change Agent. This role has some competencies that overlap with other roles they perform. However, there are nineteen competencies for the role of Change Agent that were garnered from thirty-two different resources, all of which are listed in the reference section of the work by Henschke (1991, 2002). These change agent competencies have become part of the model for the Training Division that is transforming itself into a Performance Support Division for that corporation.

The definition of a change agent is the person who possesses the ability to influence and support changes of behavior to develop and manage human capital within the organization/corporation. Following is the list of competencies and their definitions.

1. Business understanding—knowing how the functions of a business work and relate to each other; knowing the economic impact of business decisions.

2. Industry understanding—knowing the key concepts and variables such as critical issues, economic vulnerabilities, measurements, distribution channels, inputs, outputs, and information sources that define an industry or sector.

3. Organization behavior understanding—seeing organizations as dynamic, political, economic, and social systems which have multiple goals; using this larger perspective as a framework for understanding and influencing events.

4. Organization development theories and techniques understanding—knowing the techniques and methods used in organization development; understanding their appropriate use.

5. Organization understanding—knowing the strategy, structure, power networks, financial position, and systems of a specific organization.

6. Coaching—help individuals recognize & understand personal needs, values, problems, alternative goals.

7. Feedback skill—communicating information, opinions, observations, and conclusions so that they are understood and can be acted upon.

8. Group process skill—influencing groups so that tasks, relationships, and individual needs are addressed.

9. Negotiation skill—securing win-win agreements while successfully representing a special interest in a decision.

10. Presentation skill—presenting information orally so that an intended purpose is achieved.

11. Questioning skill—gathering information from stimulating insight in individuals and groups through use of interviews, questionnaires, and other probing methods.

12. Relationship building skill—establishing relationships and networks across a broad range of people and groups (cf. Emotional Intelligence Quotient (EIQ)).

13. Data reduction skill—scanning, synthesizing, and drawing conclusions from data.

14. Intellectual versatility—recognizing, exploring, and using a broad range of ideas and practices; thinking logically and creatively without undue influence from personal biases.

15. Model building skill—conceptualizing and developing theoretical and practical frameworks that describe complex ideas in understandable, usable ways.

16. Observing skill—recognizing objectively what is happening in or across situations.

17. Self-knowledge—knowing one's personal values, needs, interests, style, and competencies and their effects on others (cf. Emotional Intelligence Quotient (EIQ)).

18. Visioning skill—projecting trends and visualizing possible and probable futures and their implications.
19. Educational processes skill—ability to perform the role of change agent vis-à-vis organizations and communities utilizing educational processes.

To expand on Number 19 above, Knowles (1980, 1995), Knowles et al. (2005), Henschke (2007), and Henschke et al. (2003) provide a detailed set of the dimensions of maturation, adult education (andragogy), assumptions, and teaching technologies in which the Change Agent needs to be competent to leverage the personnel and system in getting and staying ahead of the curve in developing and managing human capital. Following are the crucial elements that need to be mastered and implemented. It is placed in articulated sections with bolding and italicizing for clarity of understanding.

DIMENSIONS OF MATURATION

The idea of maturity serving as a guide to continuous learning comes within various dimensions, each with its own unique cycle of development. If the really critical dimensions of the maturing process could be identified, then the adult educator may have some reliable yardsticks against which to measure the accomplishment of movement toward staying ahead of the curve of developing and managing human capital. There are perhaps too many dimensions of maturation to mention them all, but the following are nominated for consideration.

These dimensions describe directions of growth, not absolute states to be achieved:

- From dependence toward autonomy
- From passivity toward activity
- From subjectivity toward objectivity
- From ignorance toward enlightenment
- From small abilities toward large abilities
- From few responsibilities toward many responsibilities
- From narrow interests toward broad interests
- From selfishness toward altruism
- From self-rejection toward self-acceptance
- From amorphous self-identity toward integrated self-identity
- From focus on particulars toward focus on principles
- From superficial concerns toward deep concerns
- From imitation toward originality
- From need for certainty toward tolerance for ambiguity, and
- From impulsiveness toward rationality.

A few implications of this multidimensional theory of maturation may be as follows: Each educational activity provides opportunity for growth in several dimensions; the dimensions tend to be interdependent with one having an effect on other dimensions; and, people move from a scale of zero to infinity in each dimension of maturation throughout life, especially as the stages relate to their stage of development at that moment in time.

ADULT EDUCATION CONCEPTUAL FRAMEWORK "ANDRAGOGY": THE ART AND SCIENCE OF HELPING ADULTS LEARN

Interestingly enough, dimensions of maturation are also related to an adult education conceptual framework, especially the andragogical assumptions. One fundamental difference between children and adults is that adults have reached a maturity level both psychologically and physiologically. This maturity level has led to the important development of the adult education conceptual framework that serves as the theoretical foundations of adult learning. Below is a detailed discussion of the primary andragogical assumptions.

Assumptions: for the Conceptual Framework

Concept of the learner—As a person matures and becomes more adult in her/his perspective, they have a deep psychological need to be self-directing—to be perceived by others and treated by others as able to take responsibility for ourselves (Knowles, 1975, 1980). When we find ourselves in situations where we feel others imposing their wills on us without our participation in making decisions that affect us, we feel resentment and resistance. Educators of adult learners need to know and use the strategies that have been developed for helping adults to make a quick transition from seeing themselves as dependent learners to becoming self-directed learners.

Role of the learner's experience—As a person matures and becomes more adult in their perspective, they enter into an educational activity with a greater volume and a different quality of experience than youths. The greater volume is obvious—the longer we live, the more experience we accumulate. The difference in quality of experience arises from the different roles adults and young people perform.

This difference in experience affects the planning and conducting of an educational activity. It means that adults are themselves the richest learning resource for one another for many kinds of learning. Hence, the greater emphasis in adult education is on such techniques as group discussion, simulation exercises, laboratory experiences, field experiences, problem-solving projects, and interactive media.

The differences in experience also assume greater heterogeneity in groups of adults. The range of experience in a group of adults of various ages will be greater than with a group of same-aged youths. Consequently, adult education emphasizes individualized learning plans, such as learning contracts.

Readiness to learn—As a person matures and becomes more adult in his/her perspective, they become ready to learn when they experience a need to know or be able to do something to perform more effectively in some aspect of their lives. Among the chief sources of readiness are the developmental tasks associated with moving from one stage of development to another. Any change—marriage, the birth of children, the loss of a job, divorce, the death of a friend or relative, or a change of residence—can trigger a readiness to learn. But we do not need to wait for readiness to develop naturally. We can induce readiness by exposing learners to more effective role models, engaging them in career planning, and providing them with diagnostic experiences to assess the gaps between where they are now and where they want and need to be in terms of their personal competencies.

Orientation to learning—As a person matures and becomes more adult in his/her perspective, they are motivated to learn after they experience a need, they enter an educational activity with a life-, task-, or problem-centered orientation to learning (Knowles, 1975, 1980). The chief implication of this assumption is the importance of organizing learning experiences (i.e., the curriculum) around life situations, rather than according to subject-matter units. For example, instead of calling courses Composition I, II, III, they might be labeled as Writing Better Business Letters, Writing for Pleasure and Profit, and Improving Your Professional Communications in an adult education program.

Motivation to learn—As a person matures and becomes more adult in her/his perspective, although the andragogical model acknowledges that adults will respond to some external motivators—for example, a chance for promotion, a change of jobs, or a change in technology—it proposes that the more potent motivators are internal—such benefits as self-esteem, recognition by peers, better quality of life, greater self-confidence, self-actualization, and so on (Knowles et al., 2005). Adults may not be motivated to learn what we have to teach them. Consequently, educators of adults need to focus their efforts around how their subject matter relates to the internal motivators of adult learners that we just mentioned.

Why learn something—As a person matures and becomes more adult in her/his perspective, adults have an increasing need to know a reason that makes sense to them, as to why they should learn some particular thing—

why they need to learn the subject matter the teacher has to teach them (Knowles, 1975, 1980). Adults will expend considerable time and energy exploring what the benefits may be of their learning something, and what the costs may be of their not learning it before they are willing to invest time and energy in learning it. Therefore, one of the first tasks of the educator of adults is to develop a "need to know" in the learners—to make a case for the value *in their life performance* of their learning what we have to offer. At the minimum, this case should be made through testimony from the experience of the teacher (who needs to become increasingly a facilitator of learning) or a successful practitioner; at the maximum, by providing real or simulated experiences through which the learners experience the benefits of knowing and the costs of not knowing. It is seldom convincing for them to be told by someone (like the professor) that it would be good for them.

There is a growing body of knowledge about how adults learn and a body of technology for facilitating learning, and this is changing the role of teacher/professor and requiring that he or she know things few professors/teachers know and probably none of his or her associates knows. In working with adult learners in educational contexts the professor must know, believe in and be skillful with *andragogy*—the art and science of helping adults learn—and how it differs from *pedagogy*—the art and science of teaching youth. This is the mark of a professional adult educator.

TEACHING TECHNOLOGIES

Preparing the Learners for the Program/Course—A most common introduction to the participants of a class is sharing the purpose, objectives, meeting time and place, potential benefits, and the participatory nature of the learning design. This approach enables adult learners to develop realistic expectations about how they will be involved, and considerations of how to deal with any special needs, questions, topics, and problems.

> The first question an andragogue asks in constructing a process design, therefore, is "What procedures should I use to help prepare the adult learners to become actively involved in this course and to meet their expectations?"

Setting the climate: A climate conducive to learning is a prerequisite for effective learning. Two aspects of climate are important: physical and psychological.

Physical climate: The typical classroom setup, with chairs in rows and a lectern in front, is probably the one least conducive to learning that the human brain could invent. It announces to anyone entering the room that the rules of order are one-way transmission—the proper role for the students is to sit and listen to the professor. The effective educator of adults makes a point of getting to the classroom well before the learners arrive. If it is set up like a traditional classroom, consider moving the lectern to a corner and rearranging the chairs in one large circle or several small circles. If tables are available, place five or six chairs at a table. A bright and cheerful classroom is a must.

Psychological climate: Important as physical climate is, psychological climate is even more important. The following characteristics create a psychological climate conducive to learning (Knowles, 1970):

- A climate of mutual respect.   Adults are more open to learning when they feel respected. If they feel that they are being talked down to, ignored, or regarded as incapable, or that their experience is not being valued, then their energy is spent dealing with these feelings at the expense of learning.
- A climate with collaboration.   Because of their earlier school experiences where competition for grades and the professor's/teacher's favor was the norm, adults tend to enter into any educational activity of rivalry toward fellow learners. Because peers are often the richest resources for adult learning, this competitiveness can make these resources inaccessible. Climate-setting exercises can be used to start courses that will assist in creating a sharing relationship among learners. Do such activities at the beginning for this good reason.
- A climate of mutual trust.   People learn more from those they trust than from those they are not sure they can trust. And at this point when educators of adults (ones who seek to help adults learn) are put in a position of a teacher of adults, they are at a disadvantage. Students in schools learn at an early age to regard teachers (and professors) with suspicion until teachers/professors prove themselves to be trustworthy. Why? For one thing, they have power over students. Specifically teachers are authorized to give grades, to determine whom passes or fails, and they hand out punishments and rewards. For another thing, the institutions in which they work present them as authority figures. Professors will do well to present themselves as a compassionate human being rather than as an authority figure, to trust the people they work with and to gain their trust.
- A climate of support.   People learn better when they feel supported versus judged or threatened. Teachers of adult learners try to convey their desire to be supportive by demonstrating their acceptance of learners with an unqualified positive regard, empathizing with their problems or worries, and defining their role as that of a

helper. It will help for professors to organize the learners into peer-support groups and coach them on how to support one another.

- A climate of openness and authenticity. When people feel free to say what they really think and feel, they are more willing to examine new ideas and risk new behaviors than when they feel defensive. If professors demonstrate openness and authenticity in their own behavior, this will be a model that the adult learner will want to adopt.
- A climate of pleasure/fun. Learning should be one of the most pleasant and gratifying experiences in life; it is, after all, the way people can achieve their full potential. Learning should be an adventure, spiced with the excitement of discovery. It should be fun. Dullness is the unacceptable part of the adult learners' previous educational experience, and the professor will improve the learning climate by making a lot of use of spontaneous (not canned) humor.
- A climate of humanness. Learning is a very human activity. The more people feel they are being treated as human beings, the more they are likely to learn. This means providing for human comfort—good lighting and ventilation, comfortable chairs, availability of refreshments, frequent breaks, and the like. It also means providing a caring, accepting, respecting, and helping social atmosphere.

The second question an andragogue asks in constructing a process design is "What procedures should I use with this particular group to bring these climatic conditions into being?"

Involving learners in mutual planning—The andragogical process model emphasizes learners sharing the responsibility for planning learning activities with the facilitator. There is a basic law of human nature at work here: People tend to feel committed to any decision in proportion to the extent to which they have participated in making it. The reverse is even truer: People tend to feel uncommitted to the extent they feel that the decision or activity is being imposed on them without their having a chance to influence it.

The professor will increase learner commitment if they make clear they are coming in with a *process plan*—a set of procedures for involving them in determining the content of their study. Learners need the security of knowing that the professor has a plan, but even this process plan is open to their influence. It may be well to use teams of participants, with each team having responsibility for planning one unit of the course.

The third question the andragogue answers in developing a process model, therefore, is "What procedures will I use to involve the learners in planning?"

Diagnosing their own learning needs—At the simplest level, learners can share in small groups what they perceive their needs and interests to be regarding the acquisition of knowledge, understanding, skill, attitude, value and interest in a given content area of the course. One member of each group can volunteer to summarize the results of this discussion. This way, the learners will at least enter into the learning experience with some awareness of what they would like to get out of it. A learning need is not a need unless perceived so by the learner. It is possible to induce a deeper and more specific level of awareness by having learners engage in some of the new body of technology being developed for facilitating this process, with emphasis on such self-diagnostic procedures as in simulation exercises, assessment techniques, competency-based rating scales, and videotape feedback.

So the fourth set of questions the andragogue asks in constructing a process design is "What procedures will I use in helping the participants diagnose their own learning needs?"

Translating the learning needs into objectives—Having diagnosed their learning needs, participants now face the task of translating them into learning objectives—positive statements of directions of growth (Knowles, 1970). Some kinds of learning (such as identifying criteria for various steps in accomplishing a particular task) lend themselves to objectives stated as terminal behaviors that can be observed and measured. Others (such as decision-making ability) are so complex that they are better stated in terms of direction of improvement.

The fifth question the andragogue asks is "What procedures can I use for helping involve the adult learner in translating their learning needs into learning objectives?"

Designing a pattern of learning experiences—Having formulated the learning objectives, the professor and the adult learner then have the mutual task of designing a plan for achieving them (Knowles, 1970). This plan will include identifying the resources most relevant to each objective and the most effective strategies for utilizing these resources. Such a plan is likely to include a mix of total group experiences (including input by the professor), and subgroup (learning-teaching team) experiences, and individual learning projects. A key criterion for assessing the excellence of such a design is, "how deeply are the learners involved in the mutual process of designing a pattern of learning experiences?"

The sixth question the andragogue asks is "What procedures can I use for involving the learners with me in designing a pattern of learning experiences?"

Helping adult learners manage and carry out their learning plans—Learning contracts are a most effective way to help learners structure and conduct their learning (Knowles, 1970). Students (adult learners) contract with the professor to meet the requirements of the university courses in which they are enrolled. (Incidentally, even though there may be a number of nonnegotiable requirements in university courses, the means by which learners accomplish the required objectives can be highly individualized.) Students going out on a field experience, such as a practicum or internship, will contract with the professor and the field supervisor. Contracts may also specify how the learner is going to continue to learn on their own. Learning contracts are also used for continuing personal and professional development.

The seventh question that andragogue asks is "What procedures can I use to make certain the learners are fully engaged and involved with me in managing and carrying out their learning plan?"

Evaluating the extent to which the learners have achieved their objectives—In many situations institutional policies require some sort of "objective" (quantitative) measure of learning outcomes (Knowles, 1970). However, the recent trend in evaluation research has been to place increasing emphasis on "subjective" (qualitative) evaluation—finding out what is really happening inside the learners and how differently they are performing in life. In any case, the andragogical model requires that the learners be actively involved in the process of evaluating their learning outcomes.

The eighth question, therefore, that the andragogue asks is "What procedures can I use to involve the learners responsibly in evaluating the accomplishment of their learning objectives and meeting the course requirements?"

In conclusion, by answering these eight sets of questions, the teacher (the facilitator of adult learning, the manager) emerges with a process design—a set of procedures for facilitating the acquisition of the course content by the adult learner.

METHODS FOR IMPLEMENTING CHANGE/
MAKING CHANGE HAPPEN IN DEVELOPING
AND MANAGING HUMAN CAPITAL

In every instance where there is an external consultant working with a group within the corporation, there needs to be someone internal to the organization, or subunit of the organization, that is considered by all to be the legitimate entry point for access of the consultant into the organization. This internal person has the authority and responsibility for giving approval of the activities proposed by the consultant. The consultant also is accountable to and works through this internal person.

As a way to think about launching into change efforts, Senge (1990) shares a bit of wisdom in saying that human beings both fear and seek change. Or, one seasoned organization change consultant puts it that people do not resist change, they resist being changed.

Crawford et al. (2006) remind us that over time, companies are sustained through projects that are developed and managed by human capital. Project management successes and failures are centered around a common thread—people, or in the words of this chapter "the human capital." Thus, an enterprise is transformed by making the most of people—move toward staying ahead of the curve in developing and managing human capital.

Long (2002) also supports this idea in a bit different way, by saying that one philosophical principle is that resistance to change is a natural human attribute, but so is the will to overcome constraints and seek change. Learners encounter opposing forces to resist change and to seek change. This challenges the teacher (the change agent, the facilitator of adult learning, the manager) and the learner or worker to develop or create situations where the change state is more attractive than the static state. Risk taking frequently is touted as good, but some learners/workers have to learn to take learning (change) risks, where the consequences are controlled. Then the harm that results from failure is limited and manageable for the learner and others.

This sets the stage for the perspective of learning about change. Harvey (2001) says that we need to teach participants that individuals react to change quite differently and that these differences need to be understood and acknowledged in the formulation and implementation of major organizational change. Milstein (2001), in seeking a balance between stability and change, offers the reasoning that organizational members often dislike and fear change because they may have to deal with many unknowns and they may have to let go of cherished practices. As a result, they often dig in their heels and resist change efforts. This is aimed at helping to create a balanced image of what will change and what will not change. It is also to promote a realistic base of security while encouraging motivation for necessary changes by emphasizing what will not change as well as what will change.

Knowles (1975) suggests that the trainer/teacher/leader/agent of the change process shift from being a content transmitter to being a facilitator of learning (change) or a change process manager. Knowles (1980) explains this more in saying that the role of the role of adult educator has been changing in its basic theoretical conception: From those who teach adults—transmitter of information, disciplinarian, judge, and authority; toward those who act as change agents, performing in helping roles as helper, guide, encourager, consultant, and resource, to help learners to grow in their ability to learn (change), and to help persons become mature human beings.

McLagan (2001) adds another dimension to the essence of being a change agent. It is that if we are to have empowered actions to be the change agent we are each meant to be, we need to: Own and run a business, develop information age skills, and be our own resource manager—to step up to the plate, so to speak in a baseball metaphor, and take charge of change. Offering a simple, yet broad, perspective on change, Bridges (1991) asserts that in corporations that have successfully institutionalized the practice of continuous improvement, procedures are constantly being changed to increase production, maximize efficiency, and reduce costs. Albeit, in the situation we are currently addressing, it would be termed as movement toward staying ahead of the curve in human capital management. Little transitions or changes are occurring all the time. Without some larger continuity, everyone's world would feel like chaos. But what stays constant is the expectation that every status quo is a temporary expedient until a better way to do things has been discovered. Every one of those little improvements, though each may cause transitions, reaffirms the unchanging values and procedures that underlie continuous improvement. Endurance depends on change, as illustrated in the example that staying upright and traveling straight ahead on a bicycle depends on constant steering adjustment.

Bennett (1961) solidly observes that in organizational and group situations, the development of orderly problem-solving processes will certainly help with the change. Such processes provide a maximum participation by those affected by the change. Consequently, it is imperative for the leader to plan methods and occasions through which people can participate in the change effort. This helps the change effort to become as self-motivated and voluntary as is possible in the situation. Persons affected by the change should have as much understanding about it and its consequences as is possible. To the extent that a leader will increase ways in which they can develop and control the change, to that degree he increases the trust which persons will have in her/his leadership.

Huselid et al. (2005) identifies one major flaw to be avoided—the current human capital development and management practices that hinder employees' ability to accomplish strategic goals. To counter this they suggest that they need to meet critical needs of their workforce in terms of contribution rather than cost, replace benchmarking metrics with the ability to differentiate levels of strategic impact, and make line managers and HR professionals jointly responsible for executing workforce initiatives. All told they need to encourage the release of their most valuable asset of human capital for the benefit of the personnel, the corporation, and the constituencies they serve. An andragogical process will go a great distance in helping to accomplish this result.

Haines (2001) very candidly insists that people be involved in decisions that effect them. Lots of employees (an unlimited number) need to be involved in the key strategic and organization issues and priorities that affect them prior to implementation of a strategic plan. The focus is on the dynamic tension between ownership of the strategies for change by the leadership team and acceptance or buy-in of the plan by the key stakeholders who are crucial to the successful implementation of the desired change.

Haraburda (2007) issues a caution that in organizational decision making people's memories are flawed. They are not accurate and thus decisions based upon these faulty memories can cause significant organizational problems. Thus, program developers and managers of human capital should be cognizant of these issues and mitigate them by improving their leadership abilities, thus focusing on enhancing their human capital competence primarily in decision making.

Aubrey and Cohen (1995) characterize the successful results of change growing out of sowing and catalyzing. In sowing discomfort for results, they see the prerequisite for working at any organization they are involved with is the ability to learn (change)—which is identified as that ability to address such interview questions as: What personal or business experiences have been most difficult for you, and what did you learn (change) from them? How have you handled adversity? What are examples of important business or personal projects you have planned and how did they turn out? They indicate that sowing can be summed up in a simple gambit used by countless teachers and managers who say that they are going to tell you something that may not make much sense right now, but a time will come that it makes sense to you. Sowing and catalyzing trigger thought and action.

However, as a skill, catalyzing is different from sowing in timing and directness: In sowing, leaders and mentors sow when the time is not yet ripe, either because the learner can't yet understand what they're saying or because the time has not arrived. Catalyzing, by contrast, is a hot tactic;

it is used when change is already upon the learner, and there is pressure to quickly understand and apply new knowledge. In catalyzing, there is no previously formulated message; the meaning is in the situation itself. Catalyzing is bringing about awareness by fundamentally challenging the status quo. It is a popular and powerful tactic that uses learning and change as a learning experience (Aubrey & Cohen, 1995).

To make certain we know how difficult change is for all of us, McLagan and Nel (1995) claim that significant change in individuals and organizations involves loss, learning (change) and involvement by everyone. In organizations change comes in waves—the change maverick, the creative minority, the critical mass, the committed majority, and the competent masses. This is where the relationships between everyone become significant and have undergone a radical transformation. Successful change is like the metaphor of a bonfire. It starts with a match, which may have to be repeatedly struck (like the idea of the change maverick). The flame then moves to the newspaper (like the idea of a creative minority). The paper may have to be rekindled several times. If the newspaper burns, it ignites the kindling (the critical mass), which eventually sets fire to the logs (the committed majority), which then burn using their own resources for fuel and enabling everyone (the competent masses).

Jackson (2001) offers some hope about how to help and coach others through change, asserting that consultants need a systematic way to help clients manage change. His model identifies stages of change that employees must go through to resolve ambivalence and change behavior. Using the model, management can apply the necessary supports to help each person discover his or her own motivation for change. The six stages are pre-contemplation, contemplation, determination, action, maintenance, and recycling. Effective coaching can help people go through the change process more comfortably and effectively by giving employees what they need when they need it.

ORGANIZATIONAL GOALS AND RESULTS FROM CHANGING IN DEVELOPING AND MANAGING HUMAN CAPITAL

Knowles (1980, 1990) suggests that successful change in corporations is somewhat dependent upon having an environment of innovation, rather than having a static environment. Most people need a model for some kind of organizational transformation to take place. He proposes that if, as some say, a teacher's most potent tool, for helping to transform learners and learning, is the example of her/his own behavior (and I would add his/her own way of knowing what he or she thinks she/he knows); then, it stands to reason that an organization's most effective instrument of influence for transformation and change in human capital management is the model of its own behavior and having a grasp of its own epistemology (how it knows what it knows). An organization needs to be innovative in providing an environment conducive to the kind of learning (change) that leads to transformation into staying ahead of the curve in human capital management.

An organization is likely to succeed in transforming itself to the extent it encourages its personnel, members, and constituents to engage in a process of modeling change and growth in such dimensions as: structure, atmosphere, management philosophy and attitudes, decision making and policymaking, and communication. To be more specific, the transformation in these various organizational dimensions would be as follows (Knowles, 1980, 1990):

1. Structure—would move from rigidity to flexibility, hierarchical to collaboration, roles defined less narrowly to more broadly, being bound by property to being mobile;
2. Atmosphere—would change from task-centered to people-centered, impersonal to caring, cold to warm, formal to informal, reserved to intimate, suspicious to trusting;
3. Management Philosophy and Attitudes—would convert from controlling personnel to releasing their energy, coercion to support, low risk-taking to high, avoiding errors to learning from errors, personnel selection to development, self-sufficiency to interdependency, conserving resources to developing and using them, low tolerance for ambiguity to high;
4. Decision Making and Policymaking—would modify from participation only at the top to relevant participation by all, clear distinction between policymaking and policy execution to collaboration in both, legal mechanisms to problem-solving, decisions final to decisions tested; and,
5. Communication—would improve from restricted flow to open flow, one-way to multidirectional, feelings repressed or hidden to feelings expressed.

McLagan (2002) in researching the best practices in developing and managing human capital (organization change) learned six major lessons and numerous minor lessons supporting those major lessons and these are presented in an adapted form below. These conclusions focus on the result area. Applied to the current topic we are addressing, the result area would be movement toward staying ahead of the curve in human capital management. The research sources were journal articles and books (120 documents narrowed down from preliminary search results of more than 1200), business press, consulting/research firm reports, and worldwide web publications. The source material featured more than 35,000 organizations across 30 years; multinational, multi-industry, and multi-sector in scope; analysis conducted by scholar, practitioner, and consultant; and organization examples of practices that work. Following are the major and minor lessons.

1. Make Sure the Change Will Add Value to Your Corporation
    a. Match the Change to the Problem You Want to Solve
    b. Expect Better Quality, More Efficient, & Effective Work
    c. Expect Performance Improvement from All Personnel
2. Match the Change Process to the Challenge Being Faced
    a. Evaluate Complexity and Predictability in Workplace Activities
3. Provide Management Support for Instituting Change
    a. Clear Goals and Feedback
    b. Structure as Necessary (and No More)
    c. Invest Corporate Resources: Fund Each Project and Effort Fully
    d. Create Frequent Wins with and for All Who Are Involved
4. Prepare the Corporate System for Change
    a. Be Sure the Work Processes Are Supportive to the Work at Hand
    b. Create a Change-Oriented Management System
    c. Align the Human Resource System
    d. Find and Remove Barriers to Work Accomplishment
    e. Make Enough Changes to Ensure Success
5. Help People in the Corporation Align with the Change that is Sought
    a. Honor the Psychological Contract with Personnel
    b. Be Scrupulously Just, Fair, and Trustworthy in All Your Dealings
    c. Find the Positives for the People in Every Situation
    d. Involve Opinion Leaders Who Are Well Thought of and Trusted
    e. Communicate with All Levels of Personnel Effectively
    f. Appropriately Involve All People
    g. Ensure Skills Are Made Available and Used Appropriately
    h. Use Incentives as Appropriate
6. Create Transformational Capacity within the Corporate System
    a. Dynamically Link Present and Future
    b. Create a Knowledge Infrastructure
    c. Ensure Diverse Teams in Various Projects
    d. Encourage Change at the Work Group Level
    e. Encourage Mavericks and What They Offer
    f. Shelter Breakthroughs on Work Projects
    g. Integrate Technology with Learning and Work
    h. Adopt a New Mental Model of Organization
    i. Create an Atmosphere of Trust Throughout the Corporation.

McLagan (2002) goes on to emphasize that trust is a theme that emerges throughout the human capital development and management research. When the general climate and ambiance in and around the corporation is trusting, when formal leaders have personal credibility and are trusted, many positives are the result. Trust is such a pervasive theme that it is suggested as an important thread to weave into the fabric of the organization. And since trust takes time to build, it must be developed on a day-to-day basis so it becomes a solid and dynamic foundation supporting ad hoc and planned changes as they arise.

In learning settings this trust means that there is an operational belief in the ability and potential of the learners to understand the learning (change) process and make the right choices. The trainers (who are in the process of becoming performance support personnel, facilitators of learning/change) initiate this trust, as it takes the form of: Purposefully communicating to learners that they are each uniquely important; believing learners know what their goals, dreams and realities are like; expressing confidence that learners will develop the skills they need; prizing the learners to learn (change) what is needed; feeling learners' need to be aware of and communicate their thoughts and feelings; enabling learners to evaluate their own progress in learning (change); hearing learners indicate what their learning (change) needs are; engaging learners in clarifying their own aspirations; developing a supportive relationship with learners; experiencing unconditional positive regard for learners; and, respecting the dignity and integrity of learners (Henschke, 1998).

If all of these conditions could be met in moving toward staying ahead of the curve in human capital development and management, one natural result would appear to be fostering the 14 directions of growth needs of self-actualizing people as identified by Maslow (1970) and underscored by Goble (1971). These needs would include: (1) wholeness; (2) perfection; (3) completion; (4) justice; (5) aliveness; (6) richness; (7) simplicity; (8) beauty; (9) goodness; (10) uniqueness; (11) effortlessness; (12) playfulness; (13) truth, honesty, reality; and (14) self-sufficiency. Not only would the people benefit, but the corporations would reap a bountiful harvest. In addition, those served by the corporations would gain much.

SUMMARY

This chapter has demonstrated that changing Training Departments of corporations into Performance Support Departments focusing on workplace learning and performance is a current trend and major undertaking in today's global culture and marketplace. Critical requirements for change in the movement toward "staying ahead of the curve" in developing and managing human capital include Elements in Preparing and Planning for Change in Developing and Managing Human Capital; Required Competencies of the Change Agent in Developing and Managing Human Capital; Methods for Implementing Change/Making Change Happen in Developing and Managing Human Capital; and, Organizational Goals and Results from Changing in Developing and Managing Human Capital.

Elements in Preparing and Planning for Change in Developing and Managing Human Capital had the following insights shared: Three basic strategies of change; two responses to change; questions to be asked prior to change; strategic plans must be based upon strategic vision; need to discuss organizational change; change is about behavior and our way of knowing; providing a climate conducive to change, adaptability crucial to survival; attention to emotional and informational aspects of change; change implies risk; change may be derailed by management; strengths, weaknesses, opportunities, and threats all need analysis; and, even strategic planning in human capital management is changing.

Required Competencies of the Sub-Role Change Agent in Developing and Managing Human Capital include nineteen. Some of them were relationship building, self-knowledge, and, educational processes. The educational process was expanded to include a clear articulation of nominating 15 dimensions of maturation, and the adult education processes—andragogy: the art and science of helping adults learn. Six assumptions of andragogy were included, as were eight teaching technologies, with seven elements of providing a climate conducive to and fostering adult learning.

Methods for Implementing Change/Making Change Happen in Developing and Managing Human Capital were: external and internal consultants need to work together; humans both fear and seek change; resistance and overcoming constraints to seek change are both natural; each person reacts quite differently to change; change agent needs to shift from being content transmitter to facilitator of learning; we need to take charge of change; little changes are going on all the time; orderly problem-solving processes necessary; people should be involved in decisions that effect them; sowing and catalyzing trigger thought and action in change; change is difficult for all; and, we need to be coached through change.

Organizational Goals and Results from Changing in Developing and Managing Human Capital provided these ideas: Successful change dependent on an environment of innovation rather than a static environment; best practices in organization change yield six lessons; trust as a major requirement; and, humans and corporations would reap a great harvest and benefit from directions of growth needs being met.

CONCLUSION

Through all these discussions, one may easily come to the conclusion that continuing learning as a lifelong process in the 21st century is one of the keys to "staying ahead of the curve "in developing and managing human capital. After reading this chapter, consider whether you are in agreement with the observations and experience? I hope this chapter will stir some international debate on successfully and effectively developing and managing human capital, which is the most important asset among financial, physical and intangible assets in any organization.

REFERENCES

Aubrey, R., & Cohen, P. M. (1995). *Working wisdom: Timeless skills and vanguard strategies for learning organizations.* San Francisco: Jossey-Bass Publishers.

Bennett, T. R. III. (1961). *Planning for change.* Washington, D C: Leadership Resources, Inc.

Bridges, W. (1991). *Managing transitions: Making the most of change.* New York: Persus Books—Harper/Collins Publishers.

Caroselli, M. (2001). How to develop strategic plans based on strategic vision. In M. Silberman (Ed.), *The consultant's tool kit: High-impact questionnaires, activities, and how-to guides for diagnosing and solving client problems* (pp. 155–163). New York: McGraw-Hill.

Carrol, N. (2001). How to initiate and manage change. In M. Silberman (Ed.), *The consultant's tool kit: High-impact questionnaires, activities, and how-to guides for diagnosing and solving client problems* (pp. 124–133). New York: McGraw-Hill.

Crawford, J. K., & Cabanis-Brewin, J. (2006). *Optimizing human capital with a strategic project office.* New York: Auerback Publications.

Devane, T. (2001). Does your client's strategic plan give them the competitive edge? In M. Silberman (Ed.), *The consultant's tool kit: High-impact questionnaires, activities, and how-to guides for diagnosing and solving client problems* (pp. 24–37). New York: McGraw-Hill.

Goble, F. G. (1971). *The third force: The psychology of Abraham Maslow.* New York: Pocket Books.

Goleman, D. (1998). *Working with emotional intelligence.* New York: Bantam Books.

Hackman, J. R. (2004). *Leading teams: Setting the stage for great performances.* Cambridge, MA: Harvard Business School Press.

Haines, S. (2001). How to involve people in decisions that effect them. In M. Silberman (Ed.), *The consultant's tool kit: High-impact questionnaires, activities, and how-to guides for diagnosing and solving client problems* (pp. 134–139). New York: McGraw-Hill.

Haraburda, S. S. (2007). The seven sins of memory. *Defense AT & L Journal,* 36(1), 30–33.

Harvey, C. (2001). Learning about change. In M. Silberman (Ed.), *The consultant's tool kit: High-impact questionnaires, activities, and how-to guides for diagnosing and solving client problems* (pp. 261–267). New York: McGraw-Hill.

Henschke, J. A. (1991). History of human resource developer competencies. In J. Hinkleman, & N. Dixon (Eds.), *Models for HRD practice: The academic guide* (pp. 9–31). Washington, D. C.: American Society for Training and Development.

Henschke, J. A. (1998). Modeling the Preparation of Adult Educators. *Adult Learning, 9*(3),12–14. Washington, DC: American Association for Adult and Continuing Education.

Henschke, J. A. (2002). *Supervisor/change agent: A competency model worksheet.* St. Louis, MO: Developed for the Training/Corporate Support Division of a Major Corporation.

Henschke, J. A. (2007). *Integrating the concepts of andragogy and dimensions of maturation.* St. Louis, MO: University of Missouri. An Unpublished Paper.

Henschke, J., Cooper, M., & Isaac, E. P. (2003, March). *Teaching adults and non-traditional Conversations about teaching and technology.* Center for Teaching and Learning, and Information Technology Services, University of Missouri, St. Louis.

Huselid, M. A., Becker, B. E., & Beatty, R. W. (2005). *The workforce scorecard: Managing human capital to execute strategy.* Cambridge, MA: Harvard Business School Press.

Jackson, N. (2001). How to coach employees through change. In M. Silberman (Ed.), *The consultant's tool kit: High-impact questionnaires, activities, and how-to guides for diagnosing and solving client problems* (pp. 116–123). New York: McGraw-Hill.

Kirkpatrick, D. L. (1985). *How to manage change effectively: Approaches, methods and case examples.* San Francisco: Jossey-Bass Publishers.

Knowles, M. S. (1970). *The modern practice of adult education: Andragogy vs. pedagogy.* New York: Association Press.

Knowles, M. S. (1975). *Self-directed learning: A guide for learners and teachers.* Englewood Cliffs, NJ: Cambridge Adult Education-Prentice Hall Regents.

Knowles, M. S. (1980). *The modern practice of adult education: From pedagogy to andragogy* (rev. ed.) New York: Cambridge, The Adult Education Company.

Knowles, M. S. (1986). *Using learning contracts: Practical approaches to Individualizing and structuring learning.* San Francisco: Jossey-Bass Publishers.

Knowles, M. S. (1989). *The making of an adult educator: An autobiographical journey.* San Francisco: Jossey-Bass Publishers.

Knowles, M. S. (1990). *The adult learner: A neglected species* (4th ed.). Houston: Gulf Publishing Company.

Knowles, M. S. (1995). *Designs for adult learning: Practical resources, exercises, and course outlines from the father of adult learning.* Alexandria, VA: American Society for Training and Development.

Knowles, M. S., Holton, E. F., & Swanson, R. A. (2005). *The adult learner: The definitive classic in adult education and human resource development* (6th ed.). London, UK: Butterworth-Heinemann.

Long, H. (2002). *Teaching for learning.* Malabar, FL: Krieger Publishing Company.

McLagan, P. (2001). *Change is everybody's business.* Washington, DC: The RITE Stuff, Inc. Retrieved December 5, 2007, from: http://www.theRITEstuff.com

McLagan, P. (2002). *Success with change: Lessons from the world's research.* Washington, DC: the RITEstuff, Inc. Retrieved November 6, 2007, from: http://www.theR-ITEstuff.com

McLagan, P., & Nel, C. (1995). *The age of participation: New governance for the workplace and the world.* San Francisco: Berrett-Koehler Publishers.

Maslow, A. H., (1970). *Motivation and personality* (2nd ed.). New York: Harper and Row.

Milstein, M. (2001). Balancing change and stability. In M. Silberman (Ed.), *The consultant's tool kit: High-impact questionnaires, activities, and how-to guides for diagnosing and solving client problems* (pp. 287–289). New York: McGraw-Hill.

Myrna, J. W. (2007). *The progress pyramid.* Silver Spring, MD: Myrna Associates, Inc.

Schneider, V. (2001). Achieving a positive change climate. In M. Silberman (Ed.), *The tool kit: High-impact questionnaires, activities, and how-to guides for diagnosing and solving client problems* (pp. 347–354). New York: McGraw-Hill.

Senge, P. M. (1990). *The fifth discipline: The art & practice of the learning organization.* New York: A Currency Book Published by Doubleday.

Simmerman, S. (2001). Discussing organizational change. In M. Silberman (Ed.), *The consultant's tool kit: High-impact questionnaires, activities, and how-to guides for diagnosing and solving client problems* (pp. 233–238). New York: McGraw-Hill.

Sterrett, E. A. (2000). *The manager's pocket guide to emotional intelligence: From management to leadership.* Amherst, MA: HRD Press.

Taylor, K., Marienau, C., & Fiddler, M. (2000). *Developing adult learners: Strategies for teachers and trainers.* San Francisco: Josses-Bass Publishers.

Vega, G. (2001). Does your client's business strategy make sense? In M. Silberman (Ed.), *The consultant's tool kit: High-impact questionnaires, activities, and how-to guides for diagnosing and solving client problems* (pp. 3–8). New York: McGraw-Hill.

Wagner, S. (2001). Dealing with management resistance. In M. Silberman (Ed.), *The consultant's tool kit: High-impact questionnaires, activities, and how-to guides for diagnosing and solving client problems* (pp. 222–229). New York: McGraw-Hill.

Warner, J. (2001). *Emotional intelligence: Style profile.* Amherst, MA: HRD Press.

Watkins, K. E., & Masick, V. J. (1993). *Sculpting the learning organization: Lessons in the art and science of systematic change.* San Francisco: Jossey-Bass Publishers.

CHAPTER 2

HUMAN PERFORMANCE IN CHINA

Victor C. X. Wang

INTRODUCTION

China, the third largest country in the world after Russia and Canada, has more people than any other country with a population of approximately 1.3 billion (China Internet Information Center, 2003). China has relied heavily upon its human performance to promote desired changes in political ideology, socioeconomic relations, and human productive capabilities. To the outsiders, China's huge population could be seen as a heavy burden because feeding such a population could be its very first problem. However, the Chinese regard their huge population as a vital asset in overall economic development. Toward this end, many Chinese quote their late chairman Mao by saying, "many hands make light work." This saying has almost become the Chinese people's political motto, encouraging millions of Chinese to work harder in order to contribute to China's four modernizations, e.g., agriculture, industry, military and science and technology. According to Kaplan, Sobin, and Andors (1979, p. 126), full utilization of the country's vast workforce has been a consistent aspect of strategies to place the country on a firm economic footing. In the past between 1949 and the mid 1970s, the government was successful in mobilizing the rural workforce in support

Human Performance Models Revealed in the Global Context, pages 29–43
Copyright © 2009 by Information Age Publishing
All rights of reproduction in any form reserved.

of national development schemes. Now the government is mobilizing both rural and urban workforces to surpass countries such as Japan, Germany and the United States. As of 2006, China successfully surpassed France and the United Kingdom in terms of its GDP. After 20 to 30 years of continual economic reform, the country's foreign currency reserves reached a record $1 trillion as of March 2007, as its factories churned out goods for markets around the world, heightening the likelihood of fresh trade tensions with the United States (Goodman, 2005). The Chinese government announced the formation of a new agency to oversee investment of China's $1 trillion in foreign currency reserves, representing a potent new force in international finance (Yardley & Barboza, 2007). Although economic policies and institutions have fostered China's economic growth at a considerable rate, the efficient utilization of human resources must have played a major role in accomplishing this economic growth that has shocked the rest of the world. Speaking of human resources in China, one must turn to its definition of the labor force given its large population. Getting a clear delineation of China's labor force may be difficult simply because:

> China's mass labor mobilization campaigns obscure boundaries between those who are in and outside of the workforce. Students attend class, but they also work while going to school. Peasants farm, but can also be employed in rural and urban industries in slack seasons. Women still bear a major responsibility for housework, but millions take part in neighborhood service centers and small-scale industries. Military personnel engage in production. Thus, it is very difficult to trace with any precision the size or growth of the urban or rural, industrial or agricultural labor sectors. (Kaplan et al., 1979, p. 126)

When examining China's economic accomplishments, one immediately thinks about its mass labor mobilization in order to improve the human performance of its human resources. On the one hand, China has set a shining example for other developing countries in terms of feeding properly its huge population by mobilizing its mass labor force. On the other hand, China has revealed a plethora of problems in aggressively improving its human performance. In the next sections, I will introduce human performance in relation to labor distribution, skill and training, labor allocation and potential problems associated with human performance in China.

LABOR DISTRIBUTION AND HUMAN PERFORMANCE

Human performance refers to the end results or accomplishments desired from purposeful behavior or activity (Rothwell & Dubois, 1998). The more skilled and productive individuals are, the more valuable those individuals are to industry and commerce and, by inference, the national economy (Van Der Linde, 2007, p. 45). China's leaders have never stopped finding and formulating optimal or desirable ways of solving human performance problems or seizing human performance improvement opportunities. As soon as the Chinese communist party came to power in 1949, the future course was set as follows:

> The culture and education of the People's Republic of China are new democratic, that is, national, scientific, and popular. The main tasks for raising the cultural level of the people are: training of personnel for national construction work; liquidating of feudal, comprador, fascist ideology; and developing of the ideology of serving the people. (Kaplan et al., 1979, p. 217)

During the Great Leap Forward (1958–1959) and the Great Cultural Revolution (1966–1976), one of Mao's grand policies to improve human performance was uniting theory with practice: the direct interaction of educational institutions with productive labor and the establishment of self-supported schools by factories and commune units. Prior to economic reforms implemented in the early 1980s, the West's so-called "democratic individualism" was viewed as a key threat to improving Chinese people's performance in the work place. According to democratic individualism, the fundamental role of educating and training people for the sake of improving human performance is the physical, intellectual, emotional and ethical integration of the individual into a "complete man" (Van Der Linde, 2007, p. 42). Before China was opened to the outside world, its leaders decided that the best way of solving human performance problems was to attract foreign investment. Toward this end, the government set up many special economic development zones along its coastal provinces where China's workers, engineers and scientists could work side by side with their foreign counterparts. The goal of this historic endeavor was clear, that is, not only could China use foreign capital but also its personnel could learn advanced human management skills. During the 1980s and 1990s, the late leader Deng's theory became popular. It must be pointed out that his theory was found akin to John Dewey's pragmatism (1963, 1966). Literally translated into English, Deng's theory states: "it makes no difference whether you are a black cat or a white cat. As long as you can catch mice, you are a good cat." Applied to human performance, Deng's theory does allow China's personnel to focus on practical skills to get their work done. Further, nothing goes wrong in emphasizing skills development as a charter for education and training to meet present and future industry and economic demands (Van Der Linde, 2007, p. 48). This theory ran contrary to Mao's policy in that being "red" was more important than being "expert." During Mao's time, as long as Chinese people were loyal to the supreme leader, that was all he needed. Because of Mao's leftist policy, his theory, uniting theory with practice turned Chinese personnel into a class struggle.

Both Mao's policy and Deng's theory have contributed to disproportionate urban and rural labor distribution in China. As a result of Mao's uniting theory with practice, millions of urban youth emigrated to the countryside to improve their performance. Writing in 1979, Kaplan et al. (p. 129) indicated,

> Since the population in 1970 was estimated at about 753 million, with 125 million or 16.5% living in urban areas, this would mean that in 1975 the urban population totaled about 135 million. The rural segment therefore comprised 685 million people or 83.5% of the total population. These rations between urban and rural population have remained remarkably stable since 1958, when urban population was about 14.2% of the total. Roughly 44% of the urban population, or 59.5% million people, make up the urban labor force in 1975; a smaller percentage of the rural population—42% or 290.5 million people—made up the rural labor force.

Today, China's population remains predominantly rural, despite a strong trend toward urbanization. More than 60% were classified as rural by the 2000 census, compared with 83.5% two decades ago (Brooks & Tao, 2003). As a result of new strategies for human performance, changes in the size of the labor force largely reflect the degree to which women and young people become part of it. Because of Deng's pragmatism, changing attitudes toward female social roles also affect the size of the workforce. Now participating in economic activities outside of the home or family seems to be the norm throughout China.

SKILL AND TRAINING AND HUMAN PERFORMANCE

Writing in 2003–2004, Wang and Bott (p. 37) indicated,

> Mass illiteracy was one of the main problems facing the new government of China in 1949. Illiteracy was a serious obstacle to technical progress, both in industry and on the farm. The adult education curriculum prior to the post-Mao period in China was geared to eradicate illiteracy, and a massive assault on illiteracy became the first priority. Spare time education programs were set up for workers in cities while some literacy classes were held in the villages during those early years. Since 1984, 11 Chinese units have won prizes from UNESCO for their work in eliminating illiteracy. As a result of these efforts, by the end of the last century, China's illiteracy rate among young and middle-aged people had dropped to less than 5%.

Prior to the 1980s, the number of highly skilled workers within the industrial sector is estimated to comprise about 15% of the workforce. Most industrial workers can be assumed to be unskilled or semiskilled if wage-grade rankings are taken as equivalent to skill criteria (Kaplan et al., 1979, p. 129). According to Paltiel (1992), the Chinese pioneered the system of education and training to boost human performance as early as the 10th century AD. Prior to the 10th century AD, the Chinese philosopher Confucius, who lived in the 5th century BC, postulated that no nation goes bankrupt educating its people. As an extension of this belief, those who do well in education and training are assigned public service positions in China. And to some extent, this is still the case in China. Within the industrial sector, large numbers of workers had gone through work-study schools at the secondary level or had attended part-time courses in their factories in the 1960s and in the 1970s. As shown by Kaplan et al. (1979, pp. 129–130),

> As of June 1976, there were some 251,000 workers enrolled in high-level technical training courses in "July 21" workers colleges (named after the college at the Shanghai Machine Tools Plant cited by Mao on July 21, 1968); 900,000 workers and students in technical secondary schools; and 44.6 million students in middle schools, most of which emphasize practical production skills. In the 1970s—as an outgrowth of reforms brought about through the Cultural Revolution—many young workers just out of school have been entering the labor force with basic skills and some work experience, as well as with basic mathematical and reading abilities.

While in 1949, more than 90% of the general population—and 80% of the industrial force—was illiterate, this had changed in the 1960s and in the 1970s when China's leaders emphasized the importance of education and training initiated by the Chinese as early as the 10th century AD. Although a lot of time and energy were wasted in the political power struggle, young workers and students did master some rudimentary production skills. Indeed, the labor force in China has been transformed. In the post-Mao era, to get entry level jobs in the industrial sector, workers must have a college degree and upward mobility is most possible for those workers who hold graduate degrees. It is no exaggeration to say that the more education and training a worker receives, the better he or she will perform on the job. Work is a process going on between humans and nature, a process in which humans, through their own activities, initiate, regulate, and control the material reactions between themselves and nature (Marx, 1890/1929). More important, it is human performance that produces surplus value (Wang, 2006). Without surplus value, humans could not have progressed from Stone Age to modern civilization.

As shown earlier in this chapter, China's leaders viewed the West's so-called "democratic individualism" as a key threat to improving human performance. On the other hand, China has never stopped modeling itself after foreign human performance models. As Confucius suggested selecting members of the ruling class on the merit of individual human performance, Mao rejected formal training as the basis of his new hierarchy. Instead, he insisted on individual cultivation of moral worth as a means of inculcating revolutionary solidarity in a collective setting (Wang, 2005, p. 35). Because the Soviets were interested in indoctrinating Chinese youth with revolutionary spirit in China, Mao sent Chinese youth to Russia to improve human performance. Later, Marxist-Leninist Training Academy was established on Chinese territory. In the Post-Mao era, China's trainers began to borrow buzzwords like "system theory" and "decision-making theory" from the West. Because of China's willingness to learn from the West, more and more multinational corporations have gained a foothold to help improve human performance in China (Wang, 2005, p. 31). Likewise, going abroad to receive a foreign education to improve human performance is viewed as "realizing one's self-actualization" (Wang, 2004–2005, p. 30). In the Post-Mao era, human performance does not seem to be closely connected with politics in China. As summarized by Wang,

> Western ideas, customs and culture are much in favor, and anyone who still clings to the "four olds" (e.g., old ideas, customs, culture, habits) is considered old-fashioned. Individual aspirations for lifelong education have been stimulated by a quasi-market economy since the beginning of the early 1980s. Freed from the limitations of Mao's political agenda, motives for improving human performance have become more and more closely tied to individual, practical purposes, such as jobs, incomes, and materialistic success in life. (p. 30)

LABOR ALLOCATION AND POTENTIAL PROBLEMS

China has a history of boosting human performance by using sayings or quotes from influential people such as Confucius, Marx and Mao. Confucian thought has inspired generations of Chinese. To encourage Chinese youth to learn, Confucius twenty-five centuries ago had this to say, "Those who are born wise are the highest type of men; those who become wise through learning come next; those who are dull-witted and yet strive to learn come after that. Those who are dull-witted and yet make no effort to learn are the lowest type of men" (Chai & Chai, 1965, pp. 44–45 as cited in Wang & King, 2007, p. 253). Today, politicians and educators still use this saying to encourage young men and women in China to work hard to achieve their goals in work and in life. As soon as the Chinese communist party came to power in 1949, Karl Marx became the foremost leader in China. His ideas and concepts have been widely studied in the country. Even to this day, students are required to memorize his thought and take an exam on his thought in order to be admitted into a university or a college in China. "From each according to his ability, to each according to his need (or needs)" is a slogan popularized by Karl Marx in his 1875 Critique of the Gotha Program. The phrase summarizes the idea that, under a communist system, every person shall produce to the best of their ability in accordance with their talent, and each person shall receive the fruits of this production in accordance with their need, irrespective of what they have produced. In the Marxist view, such an arrangement will be made possible by the abundance of goods and services that a developed communist society will produce; the idea is that there will be enough to satisfy everyone's needs. While such an ideal could be realized in a pure communist country, China's leaders determined that it could not be achieved in a semi-communist and semi-capitalist country such as China. The Marxist slogan was changed into "From each according to his ability, to each according to his work." Without any exaggeration, this slogan worked to some extent to boost human performance throughout China especially in the Post-Mao China. Those who have worked harder and more intelligently in the early 1980s and 1990s gradually have become richer and richer. Those who refuse to make efforts to learn new skills have become poorer and poorer.

Today the gap between the haves and the have-nots is becoming wider and wider in both cities and in the country side. Writing in 2006, Gittings (p. 260) indicated that the fifty richest millionaires in China were worth more than Y100 million each, and the ten wealthiest among them Y 375 million and upwards, according to the Forbes Survey in 2002. On the contrary, some of the counties in Shanxi Province are among the poorest in China and many people still live in caves (Clissold, 2005, p. 28). From another perspective, Marxist's slogan (Chinese version) confirmed the Protestant ethic of work in that it was man's obligation to God to extract the maximum amount of wealth from his work (Petty & Brewer, 2005, p. 97). Since human performance is synonymous with hard and intelligent work, human performance like work should carry with it seven viewpoints that can be served as a theoretical framework when addressing human performance in any social settings: (1) human performance is continuous and leads to additional performance; (2) human performance is productive and produces goods and services; (3) human performance requires physical and mental exertion; (4) human performance has socio-psychological aspects; (5) human performance is performed on a regular or scheduled basis; (6) human performance requires a degree of constraint; and (7) human performance is performed for a personal purpose (intrinsic or extrinsic).

Regardless of what indoctrination China's leaders employ to boost human performance, underemployment and unemployment have been problems in China, especially during its first decade. On labor allocation, Kaplan et al. (1979, p. 130) reported,

Unemployment was particularly serious in the mid-1950s and immediately following the Great Leap Forward. During the First Five-Year Plan (1953–57), the unemployed were usually the less skilled, order workers, and some youths with a primary level of education. Rural-to-urban migration exacerbated this problem, so that by 1956–57 it was estimated that anywhere from 9.6 to 18.3 million people were underemployed or unemployed—roughly from one-fifth to one-third of the urban labor force. State expenditures for unemployment relief in 1956 totaled Y [yuan] 186.5 million.

During the Great Leap Forward, large masses of the unemployed were mobilized for work, including millions of women who left home to join the labor force for the first time. The problem of unemployment in China during this period was compounded when the Soviet Union decided to precipitously withdraw its industrial aid to China. Failures in agriculture brought more labor into rural industry. The so-called backyard furnace in China was a direct product of the Great Leap Forward. Labor allocation during this period caused human performance problems in China. As an incentive to boost human performance, Mao started a concerted effort to begin to shift portions of the urban population back to the countryside. This was done in China in order to achieve Mao's integration of theory with practice. Regarding education and training, the following was reported,

> Students and faculty were sent to farms and factories; curricula were formulated based on immediate agricultural and industrial needs; schools, factories, and farms shared management; classroom-centered schooling was replaced by work-study programs; workers and farmers were dispatched to take up teaching and school-management positions; and full-time and institutional facilities were increasingly replaced by part-time and non-institutional programs. (Cheng & Manning, 2003, p. 359)

In the late 1970s and early 1980s, labor was allocated by local governmental authorities who worked closely with industrial enterprises and other units in the area to ensure balance between available manpower and jobs (Kaplan et al., 1979, p. 130). At the time, China was still considered a command economy by Western standards. In the rural areas, communes and counties played the most important role in allocating labor for industry. According to Kaplan et al. (1979), these administrative levels work in close coordination with the brigades and teams, the units that manage the distribution of agricultural labor. Despite China's concerted efforts, unemployment has not been eliminated in all regions or economic sectors in China. During the past twenty years, China has made strides toward a more market oriented labor market. Toward this end, the urban private sector has grown more important and state-owned enterprises have downsized. Millions of urban workers were laid off. As rural employment has slowed, migrants have begun to seek jobs in the more dynamic coastal provinces (Brooks & Tao, 2003, p. 3). Both urban and rural employment situations have produced a new problem—surplus labor in the 21st century in China. According to the National Bureau of Statistics in 2002, an urban unemployment rate was about 4–5% of the labor force. Since more than 60% was classified as rural by the 2000 census, the unemployment rate is certainly much higher than is shown by official data. Because many of the low skill level jobs are filled by rural surplus labor, it is hard for the urban unemployed to find jobs. Since China is turning from a command economy to a market economy, nowadays, governmental authorities no longer allocate labor. Twenty years ago in China, a college degree meant a passport to a guaranteed job. Nowadays, college students with just a bachelor's degree find it hard to find quality jobs in China. Wang (2005, p. 36) noted this labor market situation in China by saying, "Numerous Chinese graduates of MBA programs at the institutions of American higher learning have difficulty finding appropriate positions in China. Some MBA graduates have taken jobs of teaching English as a foreign language for Chinese universities."

REFLECTIONS

Unlike in the West, human performance has been inextricably intertwined with China's leaders' political agenda and educational policy. Social, political, and economic conditions shape individual human performance in China (Wang, 2004–2005, p. 17). Between 1949 and 1976 when politics took precedence over educational policies, youths in China were forced to devote their time and energy, even their entire youth, to advancing authoritarian political goals. During these eras, youths' performance was not judged on their academic achievement or their occupational expertise but by how "red" they were (i.e., whether they were loyal to the supreme leader, Mao Tse-tung and the Chinese Communist Party) (Wang, 2004–2005). China has a history of creating personality cults. From its emperors in different dynasties to its contemporary leaders, all these people wanted the Chinese people to follow their "teachings" to the letter. Those who deviate from their "theories" or "policies" should be punished one way or the other and many Chinese take pride in admiring the wisdom of their supreme leaders. For example, between 1949 and 1976 when Mao wanted to create a classless communist China as a result of the class struggle, everyone's performance was geared toward realizing this political goal.

During this long period, all forms of education and formal training were sacrificed to pursue political goals under the leadership of Mao. To support its political agenda, China borrowed Marxist theories to guide human performance. As demonstrated earlier in this chapter, Marxist grand theory

"From each according to his ability, to each according to his needs" was changed into "From each according to his ability, to each according to his work" to fit the Chinese society. Like Mao, Marx became a personal cult that all Chinese youths including Chinese communist leaders worshiped throughout China between 1949 and 1976. In the Post-Mao era when national policy was geared toward economic reforms and open door policy, to some extent, the influence of Marxism and Maoism on human performance lessened. Mao's successor, Deng's theory similar to John Dewey's pragmatism inspired millions of Chinese to work harder and more intelligently in order to become rich. While hundreds of Chinese became rich overnight, some ethical standards were lost in the process of pursuing wealth in China. While Marx condemned exploitation in England Factories, Chinese rich people used the very form of exploitation to gather wealth. Millions of Chinese workers sweat in factories in order to make ends meet ($1 to $10 per day). Slave labor is rampant under the guise of realizing the four modernizations (i.e., agriculture, industry, military and science and technology). Where is the money earned at the expense of maximum human performance? It is at the disposal of a few top level leaders and their offspring. In difficult times, China's leaders are good at using propaganda and nationalism to boost human performance.

On the contrary, Westerners may not believe in China's way of exerting external control and threats to boost human performance. To Westerners, human performance is an issue related to human nature and behavior. They believe in theory X assumptions about human nature and theory Y assumptions about human nature. According to this dichotomy, some people inherently dislike work and will avoid it if they can while others consider the expenditure of physical and mental effort as natural as play or rest (Knowles, Holton, & Swanson, 2005, p. 257). Further, Westerners believe that human performance is bound by teaching/learning theories such as the theory of adult learning, the theory of multiple intelligences, the theory of emotional intelligence and the theory of transformative learning. Educational leaders such as Rogers (1951, 1961, 1969) and Knowles (1970, 1973, 1975, 1984, 1986, 1998, 2005) firmly believe that humans will exercise self-direction and self control in order to perform at the optimal level. In other words, human beings have a natural potentiality for improving their own performance. Punishment should not be the only means for bringing about human performance toward individual or collective objectives.

The essence of adult learning theory is about releasing the energy of others (Knowles et al., 2005). Therefore, human performance is closely related to self-initiated learning that involves the whole person—feelings as well as intellect—this kind of human performance is pervasive and lasting. Gardner's (1983, 1991, 1993) theory of multiple intelligences looks at the brain and how people learn to improve their human performance.

Based on this theory, human performance can be considered as an internal and biologically driven need to know for survival (Anderson, 2005, p. 3). Westerners believe that even if one's IQ is higher than the average person, one cannot perform at the optimal level if one's emotional intelligence is low. According to Goleman (2005), when a person's emotions are out of control, they can cause a smart person to act foolishly. The theory of transformative learning is useful in understanding human performance simply because this theory argues that learning in relation to perspective change other than other things is needed throughout our lifetime to help us respond to changes in the nature of work, navigate passages from one stage of development to another, accommodate new personal and professional situations (Cranton, 1994; King, 2005; Lamdin & Fugate, 1997; Mezirow, 1978, 1990, 1991, 1997, 2000; Wang & King, 2006, 2007). Such popular Western theories of teaching and learning in relation to human nature and human behavior may have been studied in the academic circles in China. However, they have not been widely applied to improve human performance in China. To some extent, human performance in China is still tied to the political agenda, national education policies, propaganda and nationalism to say the least.

CONCLUSION

It has been demonstrated in this chapter that human performance has been promoted in China by methods such as politics, influence of a few outstanding leaders, education policies, propaganda and nationalism rather than theories of teaching and learning as preferred by their Western counterparts. The chapter points out perspectives of human performance in China have changed as the political, social and economic conditions keep evolving. It was valid to pursue political goals prior to 1976 as a means of improving human performance. In the Post-Mao era, pursuing materialistic goals as a means of improving human performance seems to fall squarely in line with the seven views of human performance given China's political, social and economic conditions. Also shown in the chapter, labor distribution, skill and training and labor allocation create new problems for the overall human performance in China.

It must be pointed out that China believes in using punishment to coerce the youths into leaving poor learning behavior behind and embracing more positive and appropriate learning behavior in order to improve human performance. At the heart of this thinking is that leaders/teachers are in control of all means of improving human performance. This mode of thinking seems okay in authoritarian countries like in China. It is questionable whether it will work in democratic countries.

As problems such as underemployment, unemployment and surplus labor continue to erode the so-called "socialist" system in China, China must look for alternative ways to improve its human performance in order to result in desired changes in political ideology, socioeconomic relations, and human productive capabilities (Wang & Colletta, 1991). Toward this end, China has adopted a more flexible labor market strategy. That is, urban job-seekers are allowed to find work in the state, collective, or newly-recognized private sectors, and enterprises are granted more autonomy in hiring decisions. The authorities continue to formulate a labor plan, but instead of unilaterally allocating workers to enterprises, labor bureaus have begun to introduce workers to hiring units.

To improve training and education of the largely unskilled workers, China must introduce Western teaching/learning theories to training academies throughout China. It is important to tie training and education directly to the seven viewpoints of human performance instead of to politics, nationalism, or political agenda. "Politics takes command" should be a thing of the past. The surplus labor can be a bad thing or a good thing. If positively used, it can be turned into a productive labor force in China. The number one priority should be to provide training and retraining to the surplus labor in the country. Since they have been already exploited according to Marxist theory, training and retraining should be free.

By studying issues related to human performance and training issues in China, a totally different picture has been presented to our readers. It is not necessary for anyone to learn by heart these human performance theories and concepts practiced in China as a course of study. This chapter does provide an opportunity for our readers to use their critical thinking skills to critique, analyze and compare issues related to human performance and training issues in China with those in the United States, Europe, South America, and India in order to develop the best strategies to improve human performance to fit your organizations in your respective countries. It is by examining the acts and practices of others that we improve our own. If we adopt this as a powerful motto, we can improve human performance in any organization.

REFERENCES

Anderson, L. (2005). Applications of multiple intelligences for adult learners. In L. Bash (Ed.), *Best practices in adult learning* (pp. 3–10). Bolton, MA: Anker Publishing Company.

Brooks, R., & Tao, R. (2003). *China labor market performance and challenges.* Retrieved November 7, 2007, from: http://www.imf.org/external/pubs/ft/wp/2003/wp03210.pdf

Cheng, Y., & Manning, P. (2003). Revolution in education: China and Cuba in global. *Journal of World History, 14*(3), 359–391.

Chai, C., & Chai, W. (1965). *The sacred books of Confucius and other Confucian classics.* New York: University Books.

China Internet Information Center. (2003). *China through a lens: Population increment.* Retrieved November 8, 2007, from: http://www.china.org.cn/english/features/38109.htm

Clissold, T. (2005). *An adventurous young man collides with a vast nation on the brink of capitalism Mr. China.* New York: HarperCollins.

Cranton, P. (1994). *Understanding and promoting transformative learning.* San Francisco: Jossey-Bass.

Dewey, J. (1963). *Experience and education.* New York: Collier Books.

Dewey, J. (1966). *Democracy and education.* New York: The Free Press.

Gardner, H. (1983). *Frames of mind: The theory of multiple intelligences.* New York: Basic Books.

Gardner, H. (1991). *The unschooled mind: How children think and how schools should teach.* New York: Basic Books.

Gardner, H. (1993). *Multiple intelligence: The theory in practice.* New York: Basic Books.

Gittings, J. (2006). *The changing face of China from Mao to market.* Oxford: Oxford University Press.

Goleman, D. (2005). *Emotional intelligence.* New York: Bantam Books.

Goodman, P. S. (2005). *Foreign currency piles up in China reserve fund soared to record in 2005.* Retrieved November 4, 2007, from: http://www.washingtonpost.com/wp-dyn/content/article/2006/01/16/AR2006011600450.html

Kaplan, F. M., Sobin, J. M., & Andors, S. (1979). *Encyclopedia of China today.* New York: Harper & Row, Publishers.

King, K. P. (2005). *Bringing transformative learning to life.* Malabar, FL: Krieger.

Knowles, M. S. (1970). *The modern practice of adult education: Andragogy versus pedagogy.* New York: Association Press.

Knowles, M. S. (1975). *Self-directed learning: A guide for learners and teachers.* New York: Association Press.

Knowles, M. S. (1984). *Andragogy in action.* San Francisco: Jossey-Bass.

Knowles, M. S. (1986). *Using learning contracts.* San Francisco: Jossey-Bass.

Knowles, M. S., Holton, E., & Swanson, A. (1998). *The adult learner.* Houston, TX: Gulf Publishing Company.

Knowles, M. S., Holton, E., & Swanson, A. (2005). *The adult learner* (6th ed.). Boston: Elsevier Butterworth Heinemann.

Knowles, M. S., & Hulda, F. (1973). *Introduction to group dynamics.* Chicago: Follett.

Lamdin, L., & Fugate, M. (1997). *Elder learning: New frontier in an aging society.* American Council on Education: ORYX Press.

Marx, K. (1929). *Capital: A critique of political economy: The process of capitalist production* (E. Paul & C. Paul, Trans). New York: International Publishers. (Original work published in 1890)

Mezirow, J. (1978). *Education for perspective transformation: Women's re-entry programs in community colleges.* New York: Teacher's College, Columbia University.

Mezirow, J. (1990). *Fostering critical reflection in adulthood: A guide to transformative and emancipatory learning.* San Francisco: Jossey-Bass.

Mezirow, J. (1991). *Transformative dimensions of adult learning.* San Francisco: Jossey-Bass.

Mezirow, J. (1997). Transformative learning: Theory to practice. In P. Cranton (Ed.), *Transformative learning in action. New Directions in Adult and Continuing Education, no. 74.* (pp. 5–12). San Francisco: Jossey-Bass.

Mezirow, J. (Ed.). (2000). *Learning as transformation: Critical perspectives on a theory in progress.* San Francisco: Jossey-Bass.

Petty, G. C., & Brewer, E. W. (2005). Perspectives of a healthy work ethic in a 21st-Century international community. *International Journal of Vocational Education and Training, 13*(1), 93–104.

Paltiel, J. (1992). Educating the modernizers: Management training in China. In R. Hayhoe (Ed.), *Education and modernization: The Chinese experience* (pp. 337–357). New York: Pergamon Press.

Rogers, C. R. (1951). *Client-centered therapy.* Boston: Houghton-Mifflin.

Rogers, C. R. (1961). *On become a person.* Boston: Houghton-Mifflin.

Rogers, C. R. (1969). *Freedom to learn.* Columbus, OH: Merrill.

Rothwell, W. J., & Dubois, D. D. (1998). Thoughts on human performance improvement. In W. J. Rothwell, & D. D. Dubois (Eds.), *Improving performance in organizations* (pp. 1–14). Alexandria, VA: American Society for Training and Development.

Van Der Linde, C. J. (2007). The development of technical and further education (TAFE) in Australia. *International Journal of Vocational Education and Training, 15*(2), 37–51.

Wang, J. L., & Colletta, N. (1991). Chinese education problems, policies, and prospects. In I. Epstein (Ed.), *Chinese education problems, policies, and prospects* (pp. 145–162). New York: Garland Publishing.

Wang, V. (2004–2005). Adult education reality: Three generations, different transformation, the impact of social context, three generations of Chinese adult learners. *Perspectives: The New York Journal of Adult Learning, 3*(1), 17–32.

Wang, V. (2005). Training in China. *International Journal of Vocational Education and Training, 13*(2), 31–42.

Wang, V. (2006). A Chinese work ethic in a global community. *International Journal of Vocational Education and Training, 14*(2), 39–52.

Wang, V., & Bott, P. A. (2003–2004). Modes of teaching of Chinese adult educators. *Perspectives: The New York Journal of Adult Learning, 2*(2), 32–51.

Wang, V., & King, K. P. (2006). Understanding Mezirow theory of reflectivity from Confucian perspectives: A model and perspective. *Radical Pedagogy, 8*(1), 1–17.

Wang, V. C. X., & King, K. P. (2007). Confucius and Mezirow nderstanding Mezirow theory of reflectivity from Confucian perspectives: A model and perspective. In K. P. King, & V. C. X. Wang (Eds.), *Comparative adult education around the globe* (pp. 253–275). Hangzhou, China, Zhejiang University Press. Distributed worldwide by www.transformationed.com

Yardley, J., & Barboza, D. (2007). *China to invest its foreign currency reserves.* Retrieved November 5, 2007, from: http://www.iht.com/articles/2007/03/09/business/invest.php

AUTHOR NOTES

The following are provided to assist the reader with background on Chinese history terms.

The Great Leap Forward (1958–1959)

In 1958, Chinese communist Party and government leadership undertook the establishment of the rural people communes which, on the scale of Marxist development, moved China revolution well beyond the stage achieved by the Soviet Union (which had earlier tried and failed with a similar approach). At the same time, the Great Leap Forward movement was set in motion as vast segments of the population enthusiastically engaged in self-initiated efforts to expand production (Kaplan et al., 1979, p. 221).

The Great Cultural Revolution (1966–1976)

The Great Proletarian Cultural Revolution, a movement that was to dominate China's political, cultural and educational climate for more than a decade, began as a literary debate. Wu Han, a writer and Vice-Mayor of Beijing, had prepared a series of literary compositions focusing on the unjust dismissal from office of Hai Rui, a Ming Dynasty official who had fallen from favor because of his outspoken criticisms of the emperor. It became apparent that Wu's historical compositions were in fact intended as a veiled attach on Mao's dismissal of Peng De-huai in 1959 and on the policies of the Great Leap as well. The movement and its debates quickly spread throughout the country. The schools and universities were the initial focal points of the struggle. Within months, virtually the entire school system in China had shut down. To show support for Mao's policies, everyone in China was supposed to hold aloft the great banner of Mao Tse-tung thought and put proletarian politics in command (Kaplan et al., 1979, p. 223). Mao died in 1976 and the Post-Mao era started in China.

CHAPTER 3

PANORAMA FOR GLOBAL EDUCATION AND TRAINING OF ADULTS

A Kaleidoscopic View at the European Union Experience

Gabriele Strohschen

INTRODUCTION

The landscape of vocational education and training (VET) in the European Union (EU) is as diverse as the terrains of each of the EU's countries. It is from this landscape that the Europeans have carved out features to be incorporated into a promising preparatory and continuing adult education structure that crosses cultures and social and economic systems. A driving force in the developments that led to the Lisbon Strategy of 2000, its revisions in 2005, and the subsequent Education & Training 2010 Agenda is the goal to lead the global economy in this century. Therefore, the contemporary issues and trends of VET in Europe need to be viewed within the context of the emergence of the (ED), its geopolitical and economic agenda, and its

Human Performance Models Revealed in the Global Context, pages 45–62
Copyright © 2009 by Information Age Publishing

ideology since the 1940s. The Lisbon Agenda transpired from the special meeting in 2000 in Lisbon during which new strategic goals for the Union were crafted. The aim was to strengthen employment, economic reform, and social cohesion as part of a knowledge-based economy. As expressed by the European Council, the Lisbon Agenda has set the strategic goal for the EU "to become the most competitive and dynamic knowledge-based economy in the world" during the next decade (European Parliament, 2000, para. 5).

In this chapter I briefly sketch determining events in the history of the European Community, key principles, values, and challenges in the structuring of the European Union, and education and training trends and issues particular to the emerging EU society. I offer a kaleidoscopic lens through which to explore European values and underlying assumptions about education and training. My intent is to inculcate the discourse regarding the education of adults with thoughts that might propel a global agenda of social sustainability by means of education into our international adult education panorama.

> The year was 1955. It had been ten years since World War II ended. My world was still contained within walls that bore the pockmarks of bullet holes, and where bombed out buildings were our secret playgrounds. Most of our fathers and mothers worked in manual labor jobs. Although most of our fathers, and mothers, had received some preparatory education and training, the war had prematurely ended their study, training, and careers. The subsequent early years of the postwar economy did not open lifelong learning opportunities; nor were the majority of our parents working in positions they dreamed about in their youth. Our mothers worked in factory jobs; our fathers rebuilt the City. And we, the children of the survivors of the war, lived the illusion of prosperity and peace.

> The Wirtschaftswunder (economic miracle) peeked around those pockmarked walls of our childhood and beckoned us as we marched off to schools for our morning hot chocolate, sweet rolls, and cod liver oil pills provided by the government to Berlin's public school pupils. We learned and prepared for the forthcoming decade of the Sixties and its flourishing economy that would provide good jobs, plenty of apprenticeship opportunities, and that keenly sought after upward mobility. We valued order and structure then. We, the children of the survivors of the war, were being trained to support the vision of a new Europe emerging from the ruins.

THE EUROPEAN UNION: IMPETUS AND ORIGINS

In my hometown, Berlin, like many of Europe's cities, the Nachkriegszeit (post war period) was characterized by daily struggle for survival, particularly with the tremendous influx of refugees. Industrial plants had been destroyed or dismantled during the war. The cities heaved with the burden of rebuilding its technical infrastructure and its residential areas. The housing shortage was critical. Since the technical and social infrastructures lay in shambles, rebuilding efforts provided jobs for able-bodied women and men in the construction industries. Along with this destruction, under the surface of the rubble, the spirit of Europe's individuals and nations was low and gloomy. Once mighty conquerors had to face, openly or not, the atrocities, agony, and horror of the war; citizens of formerly proud nations had to face the fall of their nationalist institutions and the loss of status in the world. People, the every day, common ones, yearned to be part of a vision of a better future. They wanted hope.

In this social context, the seeds for European world leadership, and a post World War II version of achieving it through what would become the European Union, were sown with the proposal by French foreign minister Robert Schuman on May 9, 1950 in Paris (Alber, 2006; Dumoulin, 1988). Based on Jean Monnet's strategy to create an international initiative that would lessen the explosive potential of strong European nations' power struggles, it essentially sought to create a reconciled Europe that would emerge as a key player in deciding the world economic structure.

The first step was the establishment of a common market for coal and steel for those countries willing to delegate control of these sectors of their economies to an independent authority. This integrationist solution sought to merge western European coal and steel industries, which would result in fast economic recovery, lessen competition, and prevent future wars between Europe's arch enemies. The proposal was eagerly accepted by the first German Chancellor, Konrad Adenauer, it is said, within minutes of his reading it. In the same proposal, Schuman also projected that such an alliance would strengthen Europe's attempts in the "development of the African continent" (Schuman, 1950), providing Europe with the rationale and call for joint, global expansion in the name of social and economic sustainability in the 20th and 21st centuries:

> World peace cannot be safeguarded without the making of creative efforts proportionate to the dangers, which threaten it. The contribution, which an organized and living Europe can bring to civilization is indispensable to the maintenance of peaceful relations. (Schuman, 1950, para. 2)

Such values and ideals, particularly after the dark period of WWII, appealed to people. And Europe marched onward, ostensibly, to unite itself. The backdrop of the economic and social fabric of the 1950s offered, a sort of tabula rasa for a radical new start of regaining world leadership. Peoples of the Western European states embraced this opportunity with innovation, partnering, and by benefitting from foreign investments. Europe enjoyed the powerful support of the European Recovery Program and its economy strengthened with the gearing up for contributing to the production for the Korean War. The Eastern European states focused on industrialization and standardization. Western Europe, led by the example of the new German state, developed the structure for its social market economy, eager to find a structure that would accommodate material and social dimensions. It bears pointing out that European nations focused on creating systems that upheld social accountability and related communal support systems while inciting individual responsibility for learning, working, and growth.

Order and systems were valued; however, after the impact of National Socialist and Socialist regimes, Western Europe overtly shied away from blatantly top-down or dictatorial structures. But Europe never intended to give up its dream, albeit dreamed differently by different leaders of different nations, for regaining its status as a world power. This theme permeates the documents that chronicle the development of the EU and run counter to the development of social, political, and economic systems that will, interdependently, sustain a global society.

THE EUROPEAN COMMUNITY ESTABLISHES A EUROPEAN UNION: UNDERLYING PRINCIPLES AND PROBLEMS

Even a cursory review of the history of EU documents reveals a fundamental congruency in them about the values, purpose, and goals of a unified Europe. The EU's challenge is to "show citizens how the EU is the best tool to enable Europeans to shape globalization" (Commission of the European Communities, 2007, p. 2). The seeds that were sown by Schuman's proposal are all rooted in the desire of European leaders to regain prominence in world economic affairs. Europeans realize that economic prowess, which necessitates a competent work force, is the staple of power. Unequivocally, such documents proclaim that the "EU's raison d'etre for the 21st century is crystal clear: to equip Europe for a globalised world. We need a confident, open, reforming Europe, actively promoting the European interest. European leaders now need to maintain the vision and redouble their ambition" (EcEuropa, 2007, para. 3).

At the heart of the European agenda is "to put Europe on the threshold of a third industrial revolution" (Commission of the European Communities, 2007). The EU's processes call for a coordinated response to this challenge. Such coordination of the different values and structures of the EU member states is a reasonable and useful premise for developing a strong market system. Nonetheless, over the five decades of developing the EU, objections and power struggles have emerged. The member states, from the original six that created the European Community (i.e., Germany, France, Italy, the Netherlands, Belgium, and Luxemburg), who signed the first treaty based on Schuman's plan for central management of the steel and coal industry, needed to negotiate heartily to develop the EU and its structures as much as they have. They needed to arrive at agreements and social contracts across values and traditions, across religious beliefs, across political ideologies, and across economic interests. Perhaps most important, such negotiations bumped up against the desire for sovereignty of each member state, a value that is deeply ingrained in Europeans' longstanding tribal identities, which date to prior to the Common Era.

World affairs, civil-uprisings, wars, invasions, immigrant and refugee migrations, political overthrows, economic fluctuations, oil price wars, and terrorism over the years both threatened and strengthened the development of the EU. Some events had nations seeking the support and protection the Europaische Gemeinschaft (European Community) offered; other events pitted nations vehemently against one another. The 1992 Treaty on European Union signed in Maastricht eventually blueprinted the course for Europe to cooperate by delineating processes for foreign and security policy and dealing with justice issues. It also ushered in serious actions to establish the currency reform, leading to the adoption of the Euro by most members of the EU in 2002. A proposed European Constitution in 2004 sought to bring democratic decision-making and processes to the now 25-member strong EU. Since it was not ratified by all member states, France and the Netherlands voted against it, the EU decided to enter a "period of reflection" (Commission of the European Communities, 2006). At the time, the Eurobarometer (EurActive, 2007. para. 1) indicated that only 47% of citizens living in EU states "saw themselves as citizens of both their country and Europe, 41% as citizens of their country only." The fact that, "In general, people feel more attached to their country (92%), region (88%), city (87%) than to Europe (67%)" is said to be a contributing factor to the low voter turnout for the European parliament elections and the failure to adopt a constitution that would be the foundation for rule of law of the EU.

Each member state of the EU has to yield authority to the EU entity, which means that citizens active engagement in what is called the "long term democratic process" (European Commission, 2007a-c) is warranted to make such centralization of political processes work. The period of reflection with its so-called *Plan D,* developed in the wake of the failed ratification of a European Constitution, sought to establish a European kind of democracy through dialogue and to promote discussion among citizens of the member states to view the EU institutions and its processes as tangible, useful, legitimate, and binding.

The issue of a shared, European Identity and sense of community played a large role in the failure to ratify the EU constitutional treaty as stated above. "The point of departure of most discussions on European identity is the idea that a political community needs a common set of values and references to ensure its coherence, to guide its actions and to endow them with legitimacy and meaningfulness" (EurActiv, 2007, para. I). The suggested European values appear rather universal. The principles of the EU as delineated in Article 6 TEU are liberty, democracy, respect for human rights and fundamental freedoms, and the rule of law, clearly values that ought not be hard to embrace. At the 50th anniversary of the European Community, the Berlin Declaration highlighted the common ideals of a EU, namely, individual, human dignity and equality of men and women, peace, freedom, democracy and the rule of law, tolerance, and solidarity (EurActiv, 2007). At the same time, the fact that debates rage over the creation of a common flag and anthem is indicative that the heart of the member states' peoples still beat for their respective mother- or fatherlands. However the peoples of Europe come together over these values and principles, in spite of EU principles and because of them, their respective cultural beliefs and values, particularly within the realm of religion, continue to keep the formation of a strong European Identity at bay. The problems of the EU are largely rooted in this issue of common identity as one national community, which stumbles over strongly held cultural beliefs.

In addition to the issues of a common cultural identity and belonging to a Union in a legally binding way, issues of leadership position in decision-making power have been increasing. In 2007, the Reform Treaty, slated to be enforced in 2009 (Mahoney, 2007) is suspect by politicians, who analyze its impact on the power division within the EU's nations. Battles over voting processes in the European Parliament and control over national foreign policy, for example, continue to the present day as Europeans, standing at 27 members states in the EU, struggle to unite. Business leaders seek to protect their interests. Elected officials debate over the levels and ways in which to yield sovereignty to a EU government. Laws and processes that would centralize the sort of decision-making that go to the core of a nation's power and self-determination, such as education system, laws' governance of the labor market, and social care models, are hotly debated among the powerful, founding members of the EU and its newer, less powerful ones.

THE EUROPEAN EMPLOYMENT STRATEGY, THE OPEN METHOD OF COORDINATION, AND EDUCATION & TRAINING 2010: A PARADIGM OF VET

In 1997, the European Employment Strategy (EES) was launched at the Luxembourg Jobs Summit. It sought to reduce unemployment in Europe by 2002. At that time, a 10% unemployment rate for the EU was reported by the U.S. Department of Labor (2004). In 2004, Eurostat figures indicated that regional unemployment rates across the EU ranged from 2.4 to 32.8 percent. Needless to say, the issue of employment in Europe is connected to global economic change as Europe was losing ground on "its global competitors in growth, labour markets, skills, innovation and enterprise" (HM Treasury, 2007). National Action Plans were prepared based on the four pillars of employability, entrepreneurship, adaptability and equal opportunities.

The modernization of education and training systems, including the prevention of early school drop out, and increasing accessibility of training and apprenticeship sites through public private partnerships is foundational to these plans. Retraining and re-skilling, tax breaks for entrepreneurs, innovations in social policy to support and engage women in the labor force are among the key aspects of this approach to invigorating the labor market across the EU.

Within this context, European leaders decided to rely on the Open Method of Coordination (OMC). This OMC was created as part of an emerging European employment policy and the Luxembourg process, and it was developed during the Lisbon European Council in 2000. OMC is basically a method of governance by voluntary participation and coordination, and it is based on five elements:

1. Agreeing to common objectives for the Union.
2. Establishing common indicators as a means of comparing best practice and measuring Progress.
3. Translating the EU objectives into national/regional policies on the basis of national reports on strategies for social protection and social inclusion.
4. Publishing reports and analyzing and assessing the-national reports.
5. Establishing a Community Action program to promote policy cooperation and transnational exchange of learning and good practice (European Commission, 2007a–c, p. 2).

This attempt at voluntary governance along with the call for critical reflection is aimed at examining values and beliefs in light of a commonly shared benefit to all. For political leaders as much as the common citizen, this approach at best appeals to ideals, at worst meets with cynicism. Be that as it may, it is the process in practice for working on the development of an employment strategy and, with that, the manner in which adult education and training programs in the EU are designed and developed (Figel, 2007). In this ideal, it has merit for creating education structures around the globe that value differences and that incorporate examined practices, indigenous wisdom, and tacit knowledge into local and transnational programming as appropriate to the respective contexts.

The intent to make Europe "the most competitive and most dynamic knowledge-based economy in the world, capable of sustainable economic growth accompanied by quantitative and qualitative improvement of employment and greater social cohesion" by 2010, as laid forth in the Lisbon Strategy (Lisbon Special European Council, 2000, para. 4), continues to challenge EU member states. Moreover, the underlying concerns that had prompted the period of reflection remain unresolved, making the OMC a desirable yet effective process for renewal; that is, in the short run.

By 2006, UK Chancellor of the Exchequer Gordon Brown's critique of the European social model summed things up when he essentially called for economic and social reform, a sentiment shared by EU Trade Commissioner Peter Mandelson. The "threat" presented by the rapidly increasing education and training efforts in China and India had both men urging EU member states to re-evaluate the opportunities of global competition by analyzing internal and external forces at play. Brown put forth a threefold approach to remedy the situation:

1. Boosting productivity and competition; speeding up the process of completing the Single Market in key sectors; opening up the market for services; eliminating untargeted and distortive state aids that prevent full and fair competition; implementing proactive competition policies; and a sustained commitment to regulatory reform.
2. Skills and Employability: the development of modern social and labor market policies to help those without work find new jobs; childcare to help parents overcome barriers at work; reform of tax and benefits to make work pay; and national education and skills' policies that equip people to adapt to change work in new areas of comparative advantage.
3. Openness: Europe to take a leading role in the forthcoming Hong Kong trade talks and beyond to reject protectionism and to press for the conclusion of an ambitious trade deal that will completely open markets to exports from poorer countries (New Economist, 2005, para. 3).

These premises for reform have been criticized by Münchau (2005a,b) as politically useless, especially since the approach comes from the UK. Political positioning about whose model would help determine European economy decision continues to orbit around individual politicians' preferences and the aforementioned *tribal centricism* that lead to nation-centric judgments, like the one about the involvement of the UK in European affairs. And still, in the turbulence of creating European leadership, education and training emerged as a uniting agenda that rallied the Continental European countries as they continue to search for coordination across the wide diversity of educational institutions and traditions in the EU.

In keeping with the overall European agenda of establishing economic world leadership, education is understood to play an important role in strengthening Europe's competitive power worldwide. Aside from this, European workers, as those in the rest of the world, need to anticipate and respond to the changes that occur in the labor market. As Bertrand succinctly summarizes, a different skilled labor force will be needed in the 21st century "with more autonomous, adaptable, and polyvalent workers" (Bertrand, 1998, p. 2). Yet, what the future will require in terms of basic skills is "becoming increasingly more difficult" to identify (Luukkainen, 2000, p. 3). Based on a study by the Finnish National Board of Education, Luukkainen reports that "information related work will account for more than 60% of all occupations in working life by 2030 (2000, p. 5). And Bertrand analyzes, "The concept of competence tends to prevail on the more traditional notion of skills, as employers tend to put more emphasis on the overall competence of individuals, and especially their ability to communicate, to solve problems and to work in teams, rather than on their purely technical skills" (1998, p. 4). Bertrand insists that it is not the training of particular technical skills that will be needed but rather training is needed to enable workers for "doing the kinds of work that the technology cannot perform, i.e., those which require adaptability, creativeness and a human relationship" (1998, p. 5). Nine years later, this analysis was echoed by Joe Josephs at the Sloan-C International Conference on Technology during a plenary panel entitled, *The American Workforce in the Global Economy: The Role of Online Learning*. Josephs of the General Motors Knowledge Center and General Motors University stated that it will be the human touch and relationship building that will define the desirable worker of the future. It remains to be scrutinized why these skill sets are reemerging as desirable (Strohschen, 2007).

Ideally, the cooperation among those stakeholders, who determine the structures and processes of the markets, and the linking of educational processes across member states as much as coordinating between general education and VET structures, are essential elements for strengthening the education systems to be effective in preparing and iterative re-skilling of the workers. In Europe, the Bruges meeting in 2001 had brought together Directors General in Education to develop a process that would allow European citizens to "pursue their training needs between differing levels of education, and different occupations, sectors and countries" (Universities UK, 2007, para. 6). Then, in 2002, the Barcelona European Council vowed to make such European education and training models a world quality reference by 2010 (European Commission, 2007a-c). The Bruges-Copenhagen

Process seeks to enhance cooperation in VET in Europe. It was in 2002 in Copenhagen that 31 European countries signed a declaration to work toward opening the European market to everyone and creating a knowledge-based Europe. The objectives arising from these processes tasked European educational institutions with:

- developing a single framework for transparency of competencies and qualifications.
- implementing a system of credit transfer for vocational education and training.
- establishing common criteria and principles for quality in VET to serve as a basis for European-level initiatives in quality assurance.
- offering lifelong guidance with a European dimension (Universities UK, 2007, para. 9).

The need to coordinate across Europe's broadly diverse education systems is evident as is the EU agenda to craft processes and procedures to meet the need. Although the emphasis in the Bruges-Copenhagen process is on post-secondary education and training, such efforts need to extend to the vastly different primary and secondary education structures in the EU. Traditionally, decisions for vocational and professional career choices are made during the primary/secondary school years, and, although differentiation occurs for students at different times in different countries' education systems, Europeans tended to retrain or re-skill far less than is customary in other countries, especially North America (Bertrand, 1998). Expectations, therefore, and the willingness of individuals and employers to sustain lifelong learning within VET structures vary greatly. In the wake of this insight, the challenge is reiterated, education and training are vital for achieving the goals set by the European Council at Lisbon.

Consequently, member states agreed to work toward common objectives for their education and training systems and that their progress is to be monitored against a set of five benchmarks that are key pillars for improving education and training in Europe. It is clear that additional efforts are urgently needed to achieve the five benchmarks by 2010. "[. . .] without better education and training systems, and wider participation in them, Europe's competitiveness cannot be improved. Investment in human capital is therefore clearly a vital investment in Europe's future" (Figel, 2006).

The intent of the Education & Training 2010 agenda is to create such a "better education and training system" in the EU. The major goals to be achieved by 2010 are to improve the quality and effectiveness of EU education and training systems; to ensure that they are accessible to all; and to open up education and training to the wider world. The agenda emphasizes lifelong learning within non-formal, formal, and informed educational settings. Areas for improvement focus heavily on teacher training; basic skills development; integration of Information and Communication Technologies into instruction; efficiency of investments; language learning; lifelong guidance; flexibility of the systems to make learning accessible to all; mobility; and citizenship education.

A critical factor in bridging the education structures of the European countries is the key priority of the Education & Training 2010 objective to establish a European Qualifications Framework (EQF), which was created in 2005 and voted in just recently. This EQF "is to facilitate the transfer and recognition of qualifications held by individual citizens, by linking qualifications systems at the national and sectoral levels and enabling them to relate to each other" (Press Releases Rapid, 2007, para. 3). Through the EQF, EU citizens can access education and training throughout the EU and build on skills and knowledge previously earned in vocational training, and in academic or work settings. Other processes, like the European Credit Transfer System and Europass, support the centralization and standardization of an education and training structure in the Union to promote mobility and lifelong learning.

THE MOST PROMINENT BARRIER TO ACHIEVING GLOBAL SOCIAL SUSTAINABILITY BY MEANS OF ADULT EDUCATION: LESSON LEARNED FROM THE EU EXPERIENCE

Within these values, structures, and approaches to strengthen the success of VET in the EU, lie possibilities for a collaborative education and training system that can bridge today's multifaceted barriers to creating a structure that allows for education for all around the globe. The European Union's struggles have crystallized such barriers. Clearly, they include: lack of common identity and sense of international citizenship; lack of valuing cultures and cross-cultural understanding; insistence on maintaining prevailing educational structures and practices; political power grabbing; and the shortsightedness and shortcomings of a so-termed, traditionally Western approach regarding competition and leadership. The EU has made strides in devising ways of managing, maneuvering, and meeting the challenge to overcome such barriers by building a common agenda, and doing so slowly and collaboratively. In the European VET context, the design and assessment coordination efforts have focused on broadening access to education and training. Such access has been broadened to stakeholders with voluntary compliance and in the process, the EU has established standards and mutually agreed upon benchmarks. Moreover, the development of a VET structure rests on universally agreed upon pillars and values that, at least, open the possibilities to the sort of interdependence needed to improve the quality of life for all.

Given the method and the historical, political, and cultural context of the EU, the challenges, however, that define the EU efforts at reducing unemployment and strengthening global participation in the market eventually collided with the same sort of problems common to many nations in our rapidly globalizing, and therewith changing, era. The need for flexibility in approaches, emphasis on emotional intelligence, formal involvement of stakeholders in determining problems and solutions, international and cross-cultural sensitivity, and the need for mutually agreed upon professionalization, standardization, and accountability of VET practices remain issues in and for the EU. In spite of the easily embraced logic of a system that is based on honoring basic human values, transpositioning it into practice has been a difficult undertaking, and it is still underway in the EU. It may well be that the fundamental goal of becoming a world leader in the global knowledge-based society and its economy, by definition, derails the efforts at overcoming barriers. Based on the stated goals and intents of the EU, starting with Schuman in 1950, a vision of global community building by means of adult education is not part of the European agenda. Gaining leadership status in making economic decisions for a global world market is. And as individual member states elbow for the strongest position in the Union to spearhead this agenda, interdependent thinking, necessary for a long-term vision for education and training that leads to worldwide social and economic sustainability, is not at the core of the efforts to find solutions to the challenges.

A POSSIBLE PANORAMA FOR GLOBAL EDUCATION AND TRAINING OF ADULTS

It is precisely because of the differences that characterize each of us that we will be able to exercise the possibility of solidarity with others. And as I enter into solidarity with others, and they with me, we can combine our unique strengths to reach individual goals that, in reality, are not that different (Freire, 1995 as cited in Rossatto, 2004, p. 22). Maneuvering the landscape of VET in Europe makes for a tumultuous ride for anyone. And yet, in the structures the EU has developed along the way can be found promising possibilities for global adult education. In them, educators of adults can glimpse a vista at a future education and training structure, and find an impetus for further study and improvement. Foremost among these are:

- Standardized designs of international educational programs.

- Highly professionalized, instructional strategies that meet the needs of learners and work environments.
- Inclusion of partners/stakeholders in instructional content decisions and training in authentic practice settings.
- Relevant instruction for preparatory and recurrent education and training of knowledge workers.
- Analyses of training needs that align with organizational performance needs.
- Appropriate assessment strategies and methods.
- Leadership training that is based on both practice and research.

The processes and systems for a strong VET structure that incorporates such features have been blueprinted in the work of the EU; however, the readiness and ability of current and future employees to partake of VET offerings have not matched the intensity of these efforts. Furthermore, employers, educational institutions, both public and private, and education and training vendors approach the education and training needs with myriad philosophies, practices, and motives.

A fundamental question regarding the issues and trends of VET, in the EU as much as worldwide, remains unasked. The issues of VET are multilayered in their matrix of geopolitical, ideological, and professional frameworks. Workforce investment initiatives, generally market driven and based on a work-fIrst philosophy, leave unanswered the question as to how and whether or not they serve the needs of the adult learner (Shaw & Rab, 2003), The fundamental question is, *who will really benefit from the initiatives?* The practical and the ideological intersect in this question.

The EU has made strides in dealing with the practical. The analyses of its diverse structures have yielded insights into good practices, standards, and benchmarking of instructional quality, and of preparation and continuing professional development of knowledge workers in VET. Systems that ease access to education and training and allow transfer of credentials among different nations buttress replication. Ways of crossing cultural boundaries with sensitivity and valuing indigenous and tacit knowledge are being explored. Voluntary participation, accountability, and collaboration among stakeholders in VET have been elevated.

The ideological, which go to the core of the unanswered question, has been made clear by the EU. And, with its visibility of 50 plus years of development, the documented EU efforts provide a context for posing critical questions about the role of VET in building a sustainable world society.

In 2006, H. E. Wichit Srisa-an, Thailand's Minister of Education, opened the 10th UNESCO Asia-Pacific Programme of Educational Innovation for Development (APEID) international conference in Bangkok by insisting that people need to be put at the center of a sufficiency economy. Srisa-an implored the international audience that core concepts of sustainable development and sustainable education must be integrated into educational reform, worldwide. Moreover, he emphatically expressed his conviction that local knowledge and indigenous wisdom, in harmony with local resources, must remain responsive to global changes. If we are to achieve the goals of (a) improvement of the quality of life; (b) educational opportunity and equal access to a free quality education; (c) an Increase in educational quality and standards on all levels, as Srisa-an suggested, then partnerships are the key factor in the success of global educational reform (Strohschen Field Notes, 2006a,b).

These themes of partnerships and development by means of adult education were also at the heart of the 2006 gathering sponsored by the World Bank Institute's Global Compact Initiative in Washington, DC. "Important changes in the strategic landscapes of both non-governmental organizations (NGOs) and businesses suggest that their core objectives—profits for the private sector; local development for NGOs—can no longer be achieved unilaterally" (World Bank Institute, 2006). Simply put, then, what is shared and learned at such gatherings of stakeholders from the education, governmental, industry, and nonprofit sectors is that it does not serve us well if we are not engaging all of us stakeholders in education program design and delivery with an eye toward sustaining our world. Kincheloe (as cited in Anijar, 2000, p. ix) reminds us of the need for reaching beyond our prevailing worldview, "As comfortable ways of Euro-thinking and the stories we tell about ourselves and how we got here (the grand narratives) began to crumble, Western societies embarked on the trek to a new cultural era."

An analysis of the formation of the VET structure in the context of the emergence of the EU gives us a kaleidoscopic lens through which to view a global panorama of adult education and training. It allows us to consider possibilities and the impact of those ideologies of social and economic sustainability, which are not emphasizing interdependence. Ours can no longer be an "either-or" world as we create a global community in which everyone seeks to and needs to survive and flourish. In Sri sa-an words, we need to proceed with "honesty, integrity, and values that strengthen civil society" (Strohschen, 2006a,b). Economic and personal security through education, social justice, and the growth of our intellectual capital concerns everyone. We are interdependent. It is the profession of adult education that has a responsibility to lead the discourse on the development of VET for this dynamic knowledge-based economy in the 21st century world.

FROM THE AUTHOR

Resources for Further Study and Comparison

EurActiv, established in 1999, is a UK Public Limited Company. EurActiv "brings together the skills of professionals with-experience in EU affairs, journalism, information and communication as well as Internet technology. For its content, EurActiv relies not only on its own editorial team but also on numerous content partnerships, as well as links to the national press and the EU institutions." (Web site: http://www.euractiv.com/en/HomePage)

Open Europe is an independent think tank set up by some of the UK's leading business people to contribute bold new thinking to the debate about the direction of the EU: It includes representatives of DRAM LA SA, Wellington, Argent Group, J 0 Hambro Ltd, Shell Transport & Trading, Matheson & Co, Tribal, The Bristol Port Company, J P Morgan (Europe), Fleming Family & Partners, Gascoyne Holdings Ltd, and the IG Group. (Web site: http://www.openeurope.org.uk/about%2Dus/)

Europa: The EU at a Glance is the portal site of the European Union. It provides up-to-date coverage of European Union affairs and essential information on European integration. (Web site: http://europa.eu)

Hiemstra, R. (1995). An annotated chronology of landmarks in the history and development of adult education with particular reference to the USA. Created for the WWW, June. 1, 1995. Retrieved November 11,2007, from http://www distance.syr.edulhistorychron.htm

Imel, S. (1991). Eric and the Adult Education Act: 25 years of collaboration. (ERIC Document Reproduction Service No. ED329807). Columbus, OH: ERIC Clearinghouse on Adult Career and Vocational Education.

Knowles, M.S. (1962). *The adult education movement in the United States.* New York: Holt, Rinehart, and Winston, Inc.

Poell, R.F. (Ed.) (2000). Conference programme and abstracts of the seventh international conference on HRD research and practice across Europe, held in Tilburg, Netherlands, May 22nd–24th, 2006. Tilburg, Netherlands: Tilburg University, Department ofHR Studies.

Pollak, S. (2007). Excerpt from the Economic Opportunity Act of 1964: Findings and Declaration of Purpose. Retrieved December 5,2007, from http://www. enotes.com/major-acts-congress/economic-opportunity-act

REFERENCES

Alber, J. (2006). The European social model and the United States. *European Union Politics*, 7(3), 393–419. DOI: 10.1177/1465116506066272 Sage Publications.

Anijar, K. (2000). *Teaching toward the 24th century: Star Trek as social curriculum.* New York: Falmer Press.

Bertrand, O. (1998). Seminario sobre formación profesional y empleo. Encuentro lberoamericano de responsables de la formación professional. Trends and issues in vocational education and training: A perspective from Europe. Proceedings of the Programa de Cooperación Iberoamericana pare el Diseño de la Formación Profesional ffiERFOP. México D.F., 28 de septiembre–1 octubre de 1998.

Commission of the European Communities. (2006). *Communication from the Commission to the European Council.* The Period of reflection and Plan D. COM (2006) 212-Provisional Version. Brussels, May 5, 2006.

Commission of the European Communities. (2007). *The European interest: Succeeding in the age of globalization.* Communication from the Commission to the European Parliament, the Council, the European Economic and Social Committee and the Committee of the Regions. Contribution of the Commission to the October Meeting of Heads of State and Government. COM (2007)–581 Final. Brussels. October 3, 2007.

Dumoulin, M. (1988). La Belge et les débuts du Plan Schuman (mai 1950-fevrier 1952). In K. Schwabe (Ed.), *Die Arifänge des Schuman-Plans 1950/51. The Beginnings o/the Schuman Plan.(pp.* 271–284) Baden-Baden: Paris.

EcEuropa. (2007). *Key documents: The European interest: succeeding in the age of globalization.* Retrieved November 23,2007, from: https://ec.europa.eu/growthand-jobslkey/index_en.htm

Euractiv. (2007). *European values and identity.* Retrieved November 27,2007, from: http://www.euractiv.comlen/future-eu/european-values-identity/article-154441.

European Commission. (2007a). *EUROPA education and training.* Retrieved November 10, 2007, from: http://ec.europa.eu/education/policies/pol/policy_en.html

European Commission. (2007b). *Education and training 2010: Diverse systems, shared goals.* Retrieved November 19,2007, from: http://ec.europa/eaucation/policies/2010/back_indi_en_html

European Commission. (2007c). *The social protection and social inclusion process.* Retrieved November 29,2007, from: http://ec.europa.eu/employment_socia1/social_inclusion/index_en.htm

European Parliament. (2000). *Lisbon European Council 23 and 24 Marc 2000. Presidency Conclusions.* Retrieved December 1, 2007, from: http://www.europarl.europa.eu/summits/lis1_en.htm#2

Figel, J. (2006). *Europe's education and training: Additional efforts are needed to meet Lisbon targets.* Press releases rapid. Retrieved December 2, 2007, from: http://europa.eu/rapid/pressReleasesAction.do

Figel, J. (2007). *EUROPA Commissioner, Jan Figel homepage.* Retrieved December 4, 2007, from: http://ec.europa.eu/commission_barroso/figel/index_en.htm

HM Treasury. (2007, September 21). *Lisbon strategy for jobs and growth: UK national reform programme.* Retrieved November 30,2007, from: http://www.hm-treasury .gov. uk.! documents/intemational- issues/european_economic Jeform/int_lisbonstrategy jobs.cfm

Lisbon Special European Council. (2000). The Lisbon Strategy. retrieved August, 5, 2008, from http://europa.eu/scadplus/leg/en/cha/c10241.htm

Luukkainen, O. (2000). *European trends in anticipation of teacher training needs. Summary of answers from the Eurydice Network. Anticipatory project to investigate teachers' initial and continuing education needs.* (OPEPRO) Report 11. Project No. 98 05 16. European Social Fund and the Finnish Ministry of Education. National Board of Education and Writers.

Mahoney, H. (2007). *Unclear EU treaty provisions causing 'nervousness'.* Retrieved November 5, 2007, from: http://euobserver.com/9/25234

Münchau, W. (2005a). Economic renewal must wait. *The Financial Times.* Retrieved November 10,2007, from: http://www.ft.com/cms/s/1I63a57ae4-3e6e-11da-a2cb-00000e2511c8.html

Münchau, W. (2005b). Why social models are irrelevant. *The Financial Times Ltd 2007.* Retrieved November 10,2007, from: http://www.ft.com/cms/s/1I935e34c2-43e8-11da-b752-00000e2511c8.html

New Economist. (2005, October 17). *Gordon Brown: Old European model "not working."* Retrieved November 29,2007, from: http://neweconomist.blogs.com/new_economist/2005/10/gordon _old - euro.html

Press Releases Rapid. (2007, October 25). *The European Qualifications Framework: Promoting mobility and lifelong learning.* Retrieved November 30, 2007, from: http://ec.europa.eu/education/policies/educ/eqf/index_en.html

Rossatto, A.C. (2004). *Engaging Paulo Freire's pedagogy of possibility: From blind to transformative optimism.* New York: Rowman & Littlefield.

Schuman, R. (1950). *Declaration of 9 May 1950: Text of the declaration.* Retrieved November 18, 2007, from: http://europa.eu/abc/symbols/9-may/decl_en.htm

Shaw, K. M., & Rab, S. (2003, March). Market rhetoric versus reality and practice: The workforce investment act and access to community college education and training. *The ANNALS of the American Academy of Political and Social Science,* 586(1), 172–193.

Strohschen, G. (2006a). *Field notes.* Business, NGOs, & Development: Strategic Engagement to Meet the Millennium Development Goals. April 10–11, 2006. The World Bank, Washington, DC.

Strohschen, G. (2006b). *Field notes.* 10th UNESCO APEID International Conference on Education: Learning Together for Tomorrow: Education for sustainable development. December 6–8, 2006. Imperial Queen's Park Hotel, Bangkok, Thailand.

Strohschen, G. (2007). *Field notes.* The 13th Sloan-C InternationarConference on Online Learning. Plenary Session, the American Workforce in the Global Economy: The Role of Online Learning. November 8, 2007. Royale Caribe Conference Center, Orlando, Florida.

Universities UK. (2007). *Vocational education and training.* Retrieved November 11, 2007,from:http://www.europeunit.ac.uk/policy_areas/vocational_education_and_training

United States Department of Labor. (2004). *Unemployment rates in the European Union and selected member countries: Civilian labor force basis (1), seasonally ad-*

justed, 1990–2004. Key workplace documents federal publications. Cornell University, Industrial and Labor Relations School, Digital Commons Library. Retrieved May 31, 2008, from: http://digitalcommons.ilr.comell.edu/cgi/viewcontent.cgi?article=1068&context=key_workplace

The World Bank Institute. (2006). *Conference announcement.* Retrieved November 27,2007, from: http://web.worldbank.org

CHAPTER 4

CRITICAL HUMAN PERFORMANCE ISSUES IN THE UNITED STATES

Claretha H. Banks

INTRODUCTION

As one begins to consider critical human performance issues in the United States, one must review the historical context of human performance. Gilbert (1996) introduced the theory of human performance technology in the 1970s. Since that time many other concepts related to the theory have been introduced including: Performance engineering (Gilbert, 1978); Human Performance Enhancement (Rothwell, 1996, 2005); and Performance Consulting (Robinson & Robinson, 1995), yet they all essentially describe human performance improvement.

Rothwell, Sanders, and Soper (1999) define human performance as "the result of human effort" (p. 3). The International Society for Performance Improvement (ISPI) (2004) states that "human performance may be defined as the valued results produced by people working within a system" (¶1). Based upon these definitions, one could deduce that human performance has always been an issue within workplaces in the United States. However, we are still trying to determine the way(s) that human perfor-

Human Performance Models Revealed in the Global Context, pages 63–80

mance remains a critical function within workplace strategies in the United States. As one considers this important concern and consults the available literature on the subject, one quickly learns that there is very little empirical data that examines critical human performance issues in the United States (Carliner et al., 2006).

There are many books regarding the importance of human performance improvement, but what are they truly trying to improve? We know that human performance has consistently been at the heart of workplace activities. Work is performed to the extent that humans exert effort to complete an identified performance task. However, Bolt and Rummler (1982) noted a gap between actual performance and the capacity of an individual to perform. Recognizing that there is a gap that exists between actual performance and capacity to perform is essential to understanding the human performance issues within the United States.

Taking into consideration training reports, books and research publications related to human performance, human resource management and related literature, this author purposes the following list of critical human performance issues in the United States:

- Expanding Empirical Research to Address Issues of Hedonism;
- Training, Developing, Inspiring and Motivating Employees;
- The Lack of Consistent, Testable Models of Human Performance Improvement;
- Lack of Focus on Individual Performers to Achieve Performance Improvement Goals;
- Communicating and Measuring Value of Human Performance;
- Managing and Leveraging Resources to Reduce Resource Constraints;
- Adaptability to Change;
- Ethical Implications for Human Performance.

These issues are not listed by priority as they may or may not be as important to some human performance professionals as others due to the complexity of the area and the level of importance within perspective organizations. However, they are all vital to the success of human performance practitioners. Upon reading this chapter, one will find specific information to support why each of these issues is critical to human performance within the United States.

This chapter does not attempt to convince the reader that human performance is important to the success of United States organizations within the global economy. We know that there are many instances where society has attempted to replace human involvement with mechanical resources. These mechanical resources may remain viable to the cost effectiveness of the function of some aspects of organizational functions; yet, it has been determined that these resources cannot exist without some form of human interaction. Human interaction will never be obsolete although at times one may wish it were. According to Friedman (2005) the world is only becoming flatter and human interaction is expanding via technology.

CRITICAL ISSUE: EXPANDING EMPIRICAL RESEARCH TO ADDRESS ISSUES OF HEDONISM

Since the time of the early Greek philosophers, man has been trying to determine what motivates one to perform. The hedonistic perspective was atheoretical and was based upon the assumption that "any form of behavior could be explained, after the fact, by postulating particular sources of pleasure or pain, but no form of behavior could be predicted in advance" (Vroom, 1995, pp. 11–12). The study of motivation by psychologists has focused upon filling in this missing information of hedonism using empirical research (Vroom, 1995). However, this missing information is now being studied more in human resource development and human resource management fields.

Several empirical studies have examined the gap between HR systems and organizational performance (Becker & Gerhart, 1996; Bowen et al., 2004; Cappelli & Neumark, 2001; Collins & Clark, 2003; Delery & Shaw, 2001; MacDuffie, 1995; Reio & Kidd, 2006; Wright et al., 2005), but there are few that examine the specific lack of effort from an individual perspective. Many organizations are relying on team concepts to strengthen performance of the individual and studies have shown that teams help to increase productivity; however, team emphasis does not address the individual behavior concerns of hedonistic theory (Guzzo & Dickson, 1996).

Delery and Shaw's (2001) "model of the relationship between HR practices, workforce characteristics, workforce performance and firm performance" (p. 174) seeks to provide an answer to the gap that exists between actual performance and capacity to perform by providing a path from training to motivation, from motivation to productivity, from productivity to firm performance with indirect input from value for core competence. They also show a path from training to Knowledge, Skills and Abilities (KSAs) and continue from that point with the same path as noted above. Although this is an excellent model, there is no evidence of causality. Each of the steps is complex within itself. Empirical tests of the model need to be conducted in an attempt to provide a better explanation of how to bridge this gap. According to Delery and Shaw (2001) training and developing employees' KSAs along with inspiring and motivating them appears to be central to increasing productivity and firm performance, thus they are critical issues of human performance in the United States.

CRITICAL ISSUE: TRAINING, DEVELOPING, INSPIRING AND MOTIVATING EMPLOYEES

Training and Developing Employees

There are many methods by which employees can be provided human performance improvement instruction. Some of them include: On-the-job training, in-house classroom instruction, outside classroom instruction, job rotation, blended learning—combination of classroom and web-based learning, mentoring, and educational reimbursement. Unless the employee is trained to the extent that they have the KSA's to perform the job and are motivated to do the job, performance may be in jeopardy. As noted by Torraco (1999):

> learning and performance improvement are independent constructs; learning occurs without performance improvement and performance improvement occurs without learning. Moreover, there is no evidence that greater learning necessarily leads to better performance. However, features of the learning experience may predispose participants to better performance. Research that promises to strengthen this relationship examines the development of a climate for the transfer of learning to performance. (p. 603)

There has been consistency in the fundamental aspects of human performance. They include clarifying the tasks to be performed and the expectations of the specific tasks, continuous performance feedback provided to individuals, providing needed resources, individual motivation, managing change, leveraging diversity, and training and development of the individual to perform the desired task (Bolt & Rummler, 1982; Rothwell, 2005; Swanson, 1996). McLagan (1989) reported that the ultimate desired outcome of Human Resource Development (HRD) interventions is improvements in productivity, quality, innovation, human resource fulfillment, or readiness for change.

Human performance models and processes have been the methods of choice with which human performance professionals have attempted to achieve human performance improvement. Rothwell noted that performance "deals with the outcomes, results, and accomplishments achieved by a person, group, or organization" (p. 1). This supports the hedonistic doctrine which implies that:

> people are assumed to behave in ways that maximize certain types of outcomes (rewards, satisfiers, positive reinforcements, and so on) and minimize other outcomes (punishments, dissatisfiers, negative reinforcements, and so on). However, some of the circularity of hedonism has been overcome by the

development of more precisely stated models and by the linking of the concepts in these models to empirically observable events. (Vroom, 1995, p.12)

Gilbert (1996), who is referred to as the "Father of Performance Technology," proposed that training is incapable of dealing with every performance problem it is requested to solve. Training is designed to resolve issues related to a lack of skills and/or knowledge needed to perform a work task. Workers may possess the skills and knowledge to perform their jobs, but may lack the resources or motivation to complete their job. Gilbert also originated the term performance engineering to relate human performance techniques with regards to employee behavior to engineering concepts.

Inspiring and Motivating Employees

Human performance practitioners are being held accountable for employee performance, thus they must be able to inspire and motivate employees. Collins and Clark (2003) also found that:

> specific and general HR practices affect firm performance in different ways—specific practices seem to affect performance by building and reinforcing a specific employee-based capability, whereas general practices may affect performance more broadly through other factors such as employee skills or motivation. (p. 749)

The ultimate goal of organizations is to improve productivity through human performance, thus training, developing, inspiring, and motivating employees must remain a priority for human performance practitioners within these organizations. Reinforcing this priority consistently can only be expected to enhance human performance and subsequently organizational performance. Capelli (2005) states that "Productivity rises when employers invest in equipment and systems that help workers do their job or when workers receive more training and skills that improve their performance" (p. 9).

Amongst the comprehensive list of competencies related to human performance improvement identified by American Society for Training and Development (ASTD) (Rothwell, Sanders & Soper, 1999), inspiring and motivating employees is embedded within the leadership competency. Leadership is such a broad topic, thus inspiring and motivating employees should become a competency within itself. Human performance practitioners may take for granted that employees understand the concepts related to the various theories of motivation including goal theory, drive theory and expectancy theory. Involving employees in the development and understanding of these three theories may be the key component to improving their performance. According to Clawson and Newburg (2005), "When we *choose* to do something, we have more energy for it. When we *have* to do something, our energy is likely to flag even if we set our own goals" (p.18). Cawood and Bailey (2006) suggest further that engaged people equal enriched profits. They surmise that companies such as Southwest Airlines, JetBlue, SC Johnson, Revlon, and SAS Institute have embraced the power of the human to put the People equal Profits connection into practice daily. They propose a model that will inspire the individual and teams within organizations.

Expectancy theory of motivation (Vroom, 1995) has been used within human resource management for years to express to employees the expectations of the job. It should be expanded within human process improvement to find out what the employees' expectations are with respect to their performance and how practitioners can assist them in meeting their expectations. Expectancy theory would allow employees to explore their values and hopefully link them to performance.

Drive theory relates to the effort that employees expend on the job. Porter and Lawler (1968) suggest that drive theory views the magnitude of goal as a source of general excitement—a nonselective influence on performance.

CRITICAL ISSUE: THE LACK OF CONSISTENT, TESTABLE MODELS OF HUMAN PERFORMANCE IMPROVEMENT

Rothwell (1996) identified human performance enhancement as a step beyond traditional training and development. He introduced more than 90 forms and models to assist practitioners in enhancing human performance. This leads us to another critical issue within human performance in the United States which is the lack of consistent, testable models of human performance. Regardless of how one chooses to identify human performance, one should ensure consistency within the models and processes used to examine the concept. The United States is a free and capitalistic society which may explain why there are so many models out there that purport to explain human performance, yet provide no consistent, reliable measures of human performance. Practitioners and researchers are receiving compensation for developing models and processes to improve organizational performance while they are still trying to consistently define human performance improvement. Individuals are free to introduce new models and processes that may or may not be valid, applicable, or reliable. Carliner et al. (2006) noted that:

Despite a lack of empirical evidence, workplace learning and performance organizations are making decisions about strategic direction, job responsibilities of staff, the design of interventions, and the investment of evaluation funds based on principles that are either unfounded or that limited empirical evidence does not support or does not strongly support. (p. 87)

There is no distinct definition of human performance beyond "the result of human effort" (Rothwell, 1996), but there are many models that attempt to explain the process or how to improve it. How can one effectively improve or develop a process for something that has yet to be clearly defined or explained. Human performance practitioners and scholars must begin to work more closely together to bridge the gap between practical applications and models that have been empirically tested and are reliable.

According to Rothwell et al. (1999) in ASTD Models for Human Performance Improvement, human performance improvement is defined as:

the systematic process of discovering and analyzing important human performance gaps, planning for future improvements in human performance, designing and developing cost-effective and ethically justifiable solutions to close performance gaps, implementing the solutions, and evaluating the financial and non-financial results. (p. xxi)

Rothwell et al. (1999) also noted trends that will impact human performance in the United States including: Rapid technological change, a more educated and diverse workforce, corporate restructuring, size and composition of training department changes dramatically, training delivery is revolutionized by technology, increased focus on performance improvement, more integrated high-performance work systems, transformation of companies into learning organizations, and more organizational emphasis on human performance management. These trends were identified in 1999, yet they are still very relevant today.

Technology is continuously evolving and companies are searching for talented individuals to meet their performance needs. They are learning how to integrate more educated workers and leverage the diversity within their workplaces. Corporations are continuously restructuring to adapt to the global economy. Training departments have and are experiencing size reductions (Training Magazine, 2007). Learning Management Systems (LMSs) are being used to deliver and track training (Paradise, 2007; Training Magazine, 2007). More human performance leaders are requesting human performance improvement learning opportunities (Ringo & MacDonald, 2007). Companies are learning how to integrate high-performance work systems through the use of technology (Paradise, 2007; Ringo & MacDonald, 2007; Rivera & Paradise, 2006; Training Magazine, 2007). Learning organizations are becoming more integral to organizations and organizations are beginning to value human performance management (Paradise, 2007; Ringo & MacDonald, 2007; Rivera & Paradise, 2006; Training Magazine, 2007). However, there is still limited focus upon the complexity of the individual who is the human within the term human performance.

CRITICAL ISSUE: LACK OF FOCUS ON INDIVIDUAL PERFORMERS TO ACHIEVE PERFORMANCE IMPROVEMENT GOALS

All of the trends identified by Rothwell et al. (1999) are only as effective as the individual who may be charged to implement the trend. It is, of course, implied that the individual will be involved in the execution of these trends, but there is a lack of understanding of how to develop leaders who are capable of managing the trends. Many human performance practitioners including 92 respondents, who were selected based on the criteria of having learning budgets greater than $1 million in companies with more than 100 employees, to a survey by Lynch et al. (2007) reported that the most frequent responses identified as one of the five competencies respondents would be most interested in further learning about include: (1) Human performance improvement (53%); (2) Measurement and evaluation (53%); (3) Learning technology infrastructure (46%); (4) Strategic planning (45%); and (5) Articulating the value of learning in business terms (37%) (p. 16). Although the above items are of most interest to the respondents, there was a gap between what they found interesting and what was considered critical to their success.

> The five competencies critical to CLO success with the largest gap between most critical and most interested in further learning were: (1) Leadership; (2) Articulating the value of learning in business terms; (3) Communication; (4) Management (people, process, budget); and (5) Knowing the business of your company. The five competencies critical to CLO success with the largest gap between interest in further learning and critical to further success were: (1) Measurement and evaluation; (2) Learning technology infrastructure; (3) Learning science; (4) Human performance improvement; and (5) Research/analytical skills. (Lynch et al., 2007, p. 17)

It is rather alarming that the individuals in this research report are responsible for human performance improvement; yet, they are showing a gap in learning with regards human performance improvement. It is, however, admirable that they are interested in learning about the subject. These individuals do not lack educational credentials; however, there appears to be a divide between what they may be learning in educational institutions and their ability to function within the parameters of their particular organization.

Technology is no more effective than the person who is developing, designing, managing and/or monitoring the technology. Individuals within the workplace may be more educated and/or diverse; however, their ability to use their education within the context of the organization and to leverage their diversity to strengthen organizational performance is only as effective as they determine. Corporate restructuring is often the decision of leaders within an organization or it may be due to issues beyond their control; yet, once the decision has been made, individuals must be engaged in the execution of restructuring strategy. All of these trends are relative to the competencies that the respondents referred to as having interest in learning more about, yet they were also identified as having a critical performance gap with regards to achieving success within their positions. They essentially did not possess the skills to achieve desired success, but they also did not express interest in learning more about these issues. This does not prove that they will not learn these skills, but it speaks to the complexity of issues that must be managed by leaders within the area of human performance.

"The two most commonly cited "number one challenges" in respondents' current positions were communicating and measuring value (34%) and resource constraints (30%)" (Lynch et al., 2007, p.17). This leads to our next two critical issues.

CRITICAL ISSUE: COMMUNICATING AND MEASURING VALUE OF HUMAN PERFORMANCE

As noted by Wright et al. (2005),

> The desire of human resource (HR) practitioners to demonstrate the value of what they do for the rest of the organization has a long history. Drucker (1954) referred to "personnel" managers as constantly worrying about "their inability to prove that they are making a contribution to the enterprise," (p. 275). This has been echoed more recently by Tom Stewart, who described HR leaders as being "unable to describe their contribution *to value added except in trendy, unquantifiable and wannabe terms . . .*" (Stewart, 1996, p. 105). (p. 409)

Although it is a bit discouraging to note that the struggle to communicate and measure value is still a critical issue for human performance practitioners, we must continue to strive to address this issue. Again, it is rather difficult to communicate and measure the value of something that is not clearly defined or understood. Human performance practitioners are continuously trying to resolve this issue but must do so within constraints beyond their control. They know how to communicate and how to conduct measurements; however, determining what information to communicate and measure within complex organizational structures is difficult. For example, if human performance practitioners provide all of the safety training within a facility, yet the loss time accidents that may be reduced as a result of their efforts is reported by the safety department. The question becomes what portion of the loss time accident reduction can be attributed directly to human performance activities? What other mitigating factors contributed to the reduction of loss time accidents? Were employees provided award incentives that inspired them to work more safely? Until these types of questions can be effectively answered or determined to be insignificant to the extent that they are understood to be a value-added contribution by human performance practitioners, there will always be discussions regarding the value of human performance.

Human performance practitioners must become adept at analyzing, using, and reporting human capital data to enhance communication of their value to the organization or should they have to consistently try to prove their value when there are many organizational leaders who can "see" or perceive the value of training and other human performance activities despite the lack of specific, measurable data (Sugrue, O'Driscoll & Vona, 2005)? They intuitively know that there has been an increase in productivity since human performance activities became a priority for the organization. Organizational leaders must value human performance for what it represents to the organization and not just what they can prove. If there is no specific measurable reduction in performance or productivity since the inception of human performance activities, should one not consider it to be a valuable addition to the organization? The bottom line figure pre and post human performance activities should be a measure that is just as significant as any other in terms of its value. If all employees are trained and one measures the cost of that employee to the organization, pre and post training, one should be able to deduce whether training had a positive or negative impact on the organization's bottom line. Cappelli and Neumark's (2001) conclusions support this concept as they noted:

> most strongly supported by the evidence we obtain is that work practices transferring power to employees, often described as "high-performance" or "high road" practices, raise labor costs per employee, suggesting that these practices raise employee compensation, which represents a cost to employers. The evidence is also consistent with these practices raising productivity (sales per employee), although the statistical case for arguing that they do so is weak, especially in the longitudinal estimation. Furthermore, we generally find no effect of these high-performance work practices on labor efficiency, which we measure as the inverse of unit labor costs (that is, value of output per dollar spent on labor), although it is important to keep in mind the caveat that, statistically, a failure to find significant effects does not establish that there are no effects. (p. 766)

Ringo and MacDonald (2007) provided support that human performance practitioner perceive that there are and identified "barriers to using human capital data and information to make workforce decisions" (p. 63). Their study may not have been limited to the United States, but is relevant since it incorporated the United States. The barriers identified were:

1. Human capital systems are poorly integrated;
2. Human capital systems are not well integrated with other organizational systems (e.g., financial, sales);
3. Metrics are not well defined;
4. Inability to extract information from our HR systems;
5. HR personnel have lack of experience analyzing data in order to make decisions;
6. Quality level of human capital data is suspect;
7. Managers unwilling to access information;
8. HR personnel not oriented toward using data in decision making; and
9. Lack of executive level support. (Ringo & MacDonald, 2007, p. 63)

The report also identified possible solutions to "[i]mprove [the] ability to use human capital data and information to make workforce decisions" (Ringo & MacDonald, 2007, p. 63) including:

1. Deploying tools to make it easier to analyze human capital data and information;
2. Improving quality of human capital data;
3. Integrating/unifying human capital systems across the organization;
4. Improving definitions of metrics;
5. Educating HR personnel on using/extracting information from HR systems;
6. Providing dashboards to managers/employees to view critical performance statistics;
7. Integrating/unifying human capital systems with other systems (e.g., financial, sales);
8. Educating employees on using/extracting information from HR systems; and
9. Recruiting HR personnel with more analytical backgrounds. (Ringo & MacDonald, 2007, p. 63)

Human performance professionals may want to consider these barriers and possible solutions as they continue to explore what and how to measure and communicate the value of human performance activities. Torraco (2000) noted that human performance professionals should not brush aside learning opportunities due to the lack of outcome measures, but suggests that more attention should be given to cultivating our ability to communicate the value of learning.

Torraco (1999) also reported that although "measurement is necessary to demonstrate that performance has improved, measurement is not necessary to demonstrate the value of learning. This presents a paradox—performance improvement requires both measurement and learning; yet, rarely is learning's contribution to performance improvement measurable" (p. 608). This is indeed a paradox to human performance practitioners who are asked to show the value of learning activities via Return on Investment (ROI) strategies. The inability to measure and explain the value of learning is critical to the viability of human performance professionals within for-profit corporations and other entities.

CRITICAL ISSUE: MANAGING AND LEVERAGING RESOURCES TO REDUCE RESOURCE CONSTRAINTS

Results which reveal that human performance practitioners are facing resource constraints are somewhat unsettling when Paradise (2007) reports that:

> Growing dedication to the learning function is reflected in the increasing investment in workplace learning and performance over the 11 years we have been reporting data. [American Society for Training and Development] ASTD estimates that U.S. organizations spent $129.60 billion on employee learning and development in 2006. This amount reflects direct learning expenditures such as the learning function's staff salaries, administrative learning costs, and non-salary delivery costs. Nearly two-thirds of the U.S. total ($79.85 billion) was spent on the internal learning function, and the remainder ($49.75 billion) was allocated to external services. (p. 4)

The 2007 Training report did show that as much money was being spent as the ASTD report; however, it noted:

> Overall, U.S. organizations shelled out $58.5 billion for training this year (including payroll and training budgets), with $16.3 billion earmarked for external learning products and services. These numbers are up 4.8 percent and 3.1 percent, respectively, from last year's figures of $55.8 billion and $15.8 billion. However, growth is down compared with 2005 to 2006, when training budgets increased 7 percent, compared with 6 percent from 2006 to 2007. Approximately half (54 percent) of all training organizations reported increases in their training budgets this year versus 63 percent in 2006. (Training Magazine, 2007, p. 9)

It is evident from these two reports that financial resources are available for human performance improvement activities. A reevaluation of the use or allocation of resources and leveraging that information against organizational priorities is a must for human performance professionals. Understanding financial systems and constraints must become an essential component of the job lest we revert back to the hedonistic principle of only evaluating after the fact. Strategic planning and utilization of resources are vital to the successful achievement of human performance goals. This may be a change in the way that human performance professionals typically think about their jobs.

CRITICAL ISSUE: ADAPTABILITY TO CHANGE

The ability to adapt to change is a critical issue for human performance professionals in the United States. These professionals must be willing to change how they think about and perform their jobs. Not only must individuals be willing to adapt to change, but also organizations must be capable of changing. Torraco (1999) concluded that "performance criteria can help determine the scope and depth of learning needed to achieve system goals. This is especially important when the value of learning must be balanced against its costs" (p. 608).

Ringo and MacDonald (2007) noted that "three key capabilities influence the workforce's ability to adapt to change. First, organizations must be capable of predicting their future skill requirements. Second, they need to effectively identify and locate experts. And lastly, they must be able to collaborate across their organizations, connecting individuals and groups that are separated by organizational boundaries, time zones and cultures" (p. 2). Ringo and MacDonald (2007) also identified four themes that are globally important which are: (1) Developing an adaptable workforce—A critical capability; (2) Revealing the leadership gap—Future growth; (3) Cracking the code for talent; (4) Driving growth through workforce analytics: improving operational excellence and increasing top-line growth.

These four topics have been discussed previously; however, the adaptability of the workforce is a must within the continuously changing environment in which organizations are involved within the global economy and the speed with which technology has improved the opportunity for communication. The key points for North America were that:

1. North American firms have a strong focus on "e-enabling" HR processes and activities.
2. Companies recognize the need for knowledge transfer due to changing workforce demographics [specifically age differences].

3. HR appears less likely to play a leading role in workforce transformation because business unit leaders are in greater supply and may have more experience in leading change. (Ringo & MacDonald, 2007, p. 55)

North American firms indicated their concern with their ability to "pass knowledge along from older to younger workers (39 percent versus 28 percent worldwide) and their ability to bring new employees up to speed (39 percent versus 24 percent)" (Ringo & MacDonald, 2007, p. 59). Within the United States, the "baby boomers" have begun to retire. As they leave the workplace, they are being replaced by younger workers who lack experience and expertise to perform the jobs. In a knowledge economy, the transfer of knowledge must be successful for firms to continue to produce. Managing this knowledge has become a huge emphasis for human performance practitioners. One solution has been to hire retired workers on a part-time basis and/or as consultants. Capelli (2005) says that human resource practitioners begin a concerted effort in performance management and retain workers with the most critical skills. As the workforce ages, new human resource policies may be needed to accommodate the needs of older workers and enhance their performance within the workplace.

CRITICAL ISSUE: ETHICAL IMPLICATIONS
FOR HUMAN PERFORMANCE

Ethics have become critical to organizations in the United States as many employees have lost their pensions due to unethical decisions of those in leadership positions. Human resource practitioners are being asked to provide ethics training sessions for employees. Educational institutions are also incorporating ethics and legal issues courses into their curriculums. Darley (1996) states,

> [T]here are concrete decision options that face various individuals in the organizations, as it continues the course of doing harm even after some ethical issues become clear. These decision options generally are presented within the context of a hierarchically structured organization, business or governmental on which people are dependent for their livelihoods. Following orders, within some ill-defined sphere of activities, is legitimated, and failure to follow orders may put one's livelihood at risk. (p. 17)

As employees are faced with ethical decision-making considerations, they should feel that the culture of the organization supports their choosing the ethical decision and not one that is unethical. Employees do not want to jeopardize their livelihood based upon making the wrong decisions. According to Darley (1996) "training" is one way to socialize individuals into corruption.

> The realization that evildoing organizations have the capacity for self-replica-
> tion provides part of the explanation for one of the facts that so bewilder us
> about corporate corruption: why so many individuals are willing to participate
> in a corporation's immoral activities. One answer is that individuals in organi-
> zations are "trained" (an unfortunate use of this word) at different times, and
> those trained earlier train others, providing a multiplicative effect on the pool
> of available evildoers. (p. 38)

Human performance professionals must always consider how the culture of employee behavior has the potential to influence the behavior of all employees. Anand, Ashforth, and Joshi (2004) analyzed the impact of social context on ethical behavior. They describe how individuals tend to use rationalization tactics including denial of responsibility, denial of victim, social weighting, appeal to higher loyalties, and balancing the ledger to justify unethical behavior.

Trevino and Brown (2004) also explored the organizational context of ethical behavior and identified criteria of unethical leaders which included being a weak moral person. They describe how individuals can become desensitized to "moral awareness, ethical recognition and ethical sensitivity" (Trevino & Brown, 2004, p. 70). Human performance professionals are not exempt from these types of behavior and must be cognizant of the potential to be influenced to exhibit these types of behaviors. Organizations have codes of ethics that have been instituted to assist employees. Ensuring that they are followed is the bigger concern. Research shows that training has been effective in reducing unethical behavior, but it is only successful to extent that the individuals receiving the training use the information (Anand et al., 2004; Trevino & Brown, 2004).

CONCLUSIONS

There are many issues of concern to human performance practitioners as we continue to struggle to meet the challenges inherent in working within a global economy. According to Rivera and Paradise (2006):

> Globalization has emerged as a significant challenge for organizations that
> want to expand their learning functions outside their home countries. Orga-
> nizations that already have a robust, well-functioning, centralized, domestic
> learning function have found it very difficult to "plug-and-play" in other re-
> gions of the world. Among the most common challenges are technology defi-
> cits, adaptation to the local culture, language barriers, territorialism, conflicts

between standardization and localization, and inconsistent learning objectives across regions. Few organizations have been able to successfully globalize their entire learning functions, and have refocused their efforts on key learning function elements, particularly learning management systems. (p. 5)

The critical issues discussed here are important to the needs of today. As researchers and practitioners continue to explore this area, positive changes are expected to occur. The potential to enhance the understanding of this area and develop employees who are excellent performers is unlimited as we continue to explore these issues. Employees have and will continue to be productive within the workplace. The extent of that productivity cannot be expanded without their active participation in the process. Many methods and processes have been developed and are available for use; however, they cannot be effective without willing participants who are dedicated to achieving their expectations and those of their organizations. The complexity of human performance dictates that researchers, practitioners, and employees work together to resolve the critical issues in human performance in the United States.

REFERENCES

Anand, V., Ashforth, B. E., & Joshi, M. (2004). Business as usual: The acceptance and perpetuation of corruption in organizations. *Academy of Management Executive, 18*(2), 39–53.

Becker, B., & Gerhart, B. (1996). The impact of human resource management on organizational performance: progress and prospects. *Academy of Management Journal, 39*(4), 779–801.

Bowen, D. E., & Ostroff, C. (2004). Understanding HRM–firm performance linkages: The role of the "strength" of the HRM system. *Academy of Management Review, 29*(2), 203–221.

Bolt, J. E, & Rummler, G. A. (1982). How to close the gap in human performance. *Management Review, 71*(1), 38–44.

Capelli, P. (2005). Will there really be a labor shortage? In M. Losey, S. Meisinger, & D. Ulrich (Eds.), *The future of human resource management: 64 thought leaders explore the critical HR issues of today and tomorrow* (pp.15–22). Hoboken, NJ: John Wiley & Sons, Inc.

Cappelli, P., & Neumark, D. (2001). Do "high-performance" work practices improve establishment-level outcomes? *Industrial and Labor Relations Review, 54*(4), 737–775.

Carliner, S., Ally, M., Zhao, N., Bairstow, L., Khoury, S., & Johnston, L. (2006). *A review of the state of the field of workplace learning: What we know and what we need to know about competencies, diversity, e-learning, and human performance improvement.* Toronto: Canadian Society for Training and Development.

Cawood, S., & Bailey, R. V. (2006). *Destination profit: Creating people-profit opportunities in your organization.* Mountain View, CA: Davies-Black Publishing.

Clawson, J. G., & Newburg, D. (2005). The motivator's dilemma. In M. Losey, S. Meisinger, & D. Ulrich (Eds.), *The future of human resource management: 64 thought leaders explore the critical HR issues of today and tomorrow* (pp.15–22). Hoboken, NJ: John Wiley & Sons, Inc.

Collins, C. J., & Clark, K. D. (2003). Strategic human resource practices, top management team social networks, and firm performance: The role of human resource practices in creating organizational competitive advantage. *Academy of Management Journal, 46*(6), 740–751.

Darley, J. M. (1996). How organizations socialize individuals into evildoing. In D. M. Messick, & A. E. Tenbrunsel (Eds.), *Codes of conduct: Behavioral research into business ethics* (pp. 13–43). New York: Russell Sage Foundation.

Delery, J. E., & Shaw, J. D. (2001). The strategic management of people in work organizations: Review, synthesis and extension. In G. R. Ferris (Ed.), *Research in personnel and human resource management* (Vol. 20, pp. 167–197). New York: JAI Press.

Drucker P. (1954). *The practice of management.* New York: Harper & Row.

Freidman, T. (2005). *The world is flat.* New York: Farrar, Straus & Giroux.

Gilbert, T. F. (1978). *Human competence: Engineering worthy performance.* New York: McGraw Hill.

Gilbert, T. (1996.) *Human competence: Engineering worthy performance* (*ISPI tribute ed.*). Silver Spring, MD: International Society for Performance Improvement.

Guzzo, R. A., & Dickson, M. W. (1996). Teams in organizations: Recent research on performance and effectiveness. *Annual Review of Psychology, 47,* 307–338.

International Society for Performance Improvement (ISPI). (2004, May). *Author guidelines: Performance improvement quarterly author guidelines.* Retrieved December 30, 2007, from: http://www.ispi.org/publications/PIQ_AuthorGuidelines.pdf

Lynch, D., Sugrue, B., Rivera R., & Betof, A. (2007). *Learning executive profile research report.* Alexandria, VA: ASTD/University of Pennsylvania.

MacDuffie, J. P. (1995). Human resource bundles and manufacturing performance: Organizational logic and flexible production systems in the world auto industry. *Industrial and Labor Relations Review, 48*(2), 197–221.

McLagan, P. (1989). *The models. A volume in models for HRD practice.* Alexandria, VA: American Society for Training and Development.

Paradise, A. (2007). *State of the industry: ASTD's annual review of trends in workplace learning and performance.* Alexandria, VA: ASTD.

Porter, L. W., & Lawler, E. E. (1968). *Managerial attitudes and performance.* Homewood, IL: Richard D. Irwin, Inc.

Reio, R. G., & Kidd, C. A. (2006). An exploration of the impact of employee job satisfaction, affect, job performance, and organizational financial performance: A review of the literature. In F. M. Nafukho, & H. C. Chen (Eds.), *Proceedings Academy of Human Resource Development 2006 International Conference* (pp. 355–362). Bowling Green, KY: Academy of Human Resource Development.

Ringo, T., & McDonald, R. (2007*). Unlocking the DNA of the adaptable workforce: The global human capital study 2008.* Somers, NY: IBM Global Services.

Rivera, R., & Paradise, A. (2006). *State of the industry in leading enterprises: ASTD's annual review of trends in workplace learning and performance.* Alexandria, VA: American Society for Training and Development.

Robinson, D. G., & Robinson, J. C. (1995). *Performance consulting: Moving beyond training.* San Francisco: Berrett-Koehler.

Rothwell, W. J. (1996). *Beyond training and development: State-of-the-Art strategies for enhancing human performance.* New York: AMACOM.

Rothwell W. J. (2005). *Beyond training and development: The groundbreaking classic on human performance enhancement.* New York: AMACOM.

Rothwell, W. J., Hohne, C., & King, S. B. (2007). *Human performance improvement: Building practitioner competence* (2nd ed). Burlington, MA: Elsevier.

Rothwell, W. J., Sanders, E. S., & Soper, J.G. (1999). *ASTD models for human performance improvement.* Alexandria, VA: American Society for Training and Development.

Stewart T. (1996). Taking on the last bureaucracy. *Fortune, 133*(1), 105, 106, 108.

Sugrue, B., O'Driscoll, T., & Vona, M. K. (2005.) The C-level and the value of learning. *Training & Development, 59*(10), 70–78.

Swanson, R. A. (1996). *Analysis for improving performance: Tools for diagnosing organizations and documenting workplace expertise.* San Francisco: Berrett-Koehler Publishers.

Toracco, R. J. (1999). The relationship of learning and performance improvement at different system levels. In K. P. Kuchinke (Ed.), *Proceedings of the 1999 AHRD Conference* (pp. 602–610). Baton Rouge, LA: Academy of Human Resource Development.

Torraco, R. J. (2000). The relationship of learning and performance improvement at different system levels. *Performance Improvement Quarterly, 13*(1), 60–83.

Training Magazine. (2007, November/December). *2007 Training industry report: Training Magazine's exclusive analysis of the U.S. training industry.* Retrieved December 29, 2007, from: http://www.trainingmag.com/msg/content_display/publications/
e3ib4fbcf3a3d03c749a6b1d043938e5a4d.

Trevino, L. K., & Brown, M.E. (2004). Managing to be ethical: Debunking five business ethics myths. *Academy of Management Executive, 16*(3), 69–81.

Vroom, V. H. (1995). *Work and motivation.* San Francisco: Jossey-Bass.

Wright, P. M., Gardner, T. M., Moynihan, L.M., & Allen, M. R. (2005). The relationship between HR practices and firm performance: Examining causal order. *Personnel Psychology 58*(2), 409–446.

CHAPTER 5

PERFORMANCE CONTRACTING AND HUMAN PERFORMANCE PRACTICES IN AFRICA

Fredrick Muyia Nafukho, Margaret Kobia, and Nura M. Huka

INTRODUCTION

A major issue in human resource development is determining factors that predict the performance of employees whether in a public setting or in a private corporate environment. Performance is used in general terms to refer to societal performance, organizational performance, team performance, and individual performance. In this chapter, performance focuses on the individual and the processes put in place by several African countries as a strategy to improve human performance and by extension, the performance of the public service, a major employer of people in Africa. First, the chapter is devoted to examining the meaning of performance. This is followed by the explanation of a new phenomenon in the area of human performance—performance contracting, and how it is currently being employed in Africa to increase the productivity of employees. Also examined

Human Performance Models Revealed in the Global Context, pages 81–102
Copyright © 2009 by Information Age Publishing
81

in the chapter are the failures and successes of performance contracting processes in promoting human performance. Several case studies are utilized in the chapter to support the rationale for performance contracting in Africa as a strategy for optimizing human potential and promoting the productivity of African economies. Kenya is used in this chapter to illustrate the use of performance contracting in Africa.

MEANING OF PERFORMANCE

The primary theoretical framework of this study is grounded in the empirical research on performance improvement literature. A number of theories that attempt to explain how work conditions impact performance at the workplace have been developed. According to Rotter (1982), to understand behavior, one must study both the individual and the work environment. Thus, Rotter identifies the main elements that predict performance. These are Behavior Potential (BP), Expectancy (E) and Reinforcement Value (RV) which can be combined into a predictive formula for behavior: $BP = f (E \& RV)$. This can be interpreted as follows: behavior potential is a function of expectancy and reinforcement value. The likelihood of a person exhibiting a particular behavior is a function of the probability that behavior will lead to a given outcome and the desirability of that outcome. If expectancy and reinforcement value are both high, then behavior potential will be high. If either expectancy or reinforcement value is low, then behavior potential will be lower. Expectancy theory states that behavior is a function of the value of a reward and the expectancy of achieving the reward (Steinmetz & Todd, 1992). Performance (P) is the result of the interaction of two components; force (F) and ability (A), with ability representing the potential for performing some tasks (Vroom, 1964). The force to perform an act is the algebraic sum of the products of the valences of all outcomes (E) and the valence or rewards of those outcomes (V). This can be expressed symbolically as: "$P = (F \times A)$" (Yamnill & McLean, 2001, p. 196).

PERFORMANCE IMPROVEMENT (PI)

Having looked at the meaning of performance, it is important that we examine another important term associated with performance—performance improvement (PI). Thus, PI is broader than any single set of theoretical practices since most successful strategies for system and subsystem improvement require multidisciplinary interventions. The theory of improvement derives from multiple theories (Swanson, 1999). Rummler and Brache (1995) noted that performance improvement consists of organizational, process and individual levels. While Swanson (1999) advanced a theoretical foundation of performance improvement, in his theory of PI, he noted that it comprises economic theory, psychological theory, and systems theory. In addition, he argued that ethics was the glue that held the three theories of PI together. According to Swanson (1999) the psychological theory recognizes the fact that PI takes place in organizations that are psychologically framed by those who founded them, operate in them, and renew them.

Systems theory is relevant to performance improvement since performance issues take place in organizations that are themselves systems with subsystems functioning within an ever changing environmental system (Gradous, 1989; Swanson, 1999). "Every purposefully organized system operates either explicitly or implicitly with a mission and the role of the mission is to reflect the system's relationship with the external environment" (Holton, 1999, p. 29).

Performance factors that can be manipulated to enhance organizational, group, or individual performance levels include consequences, incentives and rewards; the feedback and standards of performance; individual capacity, the capabilities of an individual's performance, and motives and expectations, skills and knowledge that employees hold (Gilbert, 1978, 1988, 1996; Rummler & Brache, 1995; Swanson & Arnold, 1997; Weinberger, 1998). This then shows the importance of performance contracting as a strategy to guide both employers and employees at the work place.

WHAT IS PERFORMANCE CONTRACTING?

Several definitions of performance contracting exist. For the purpose of this chapter, performance contracting can be defined as "a branch of management science referred to as Management Control Systems" (Kobia & Huka, 2006, p. 4). According to Kenya Sensitization Training Manual (Government of Kenya, GOK, 2005b), a performance contract is a freely negotiated performance agreement between government, organizations and individuals. It is an agreement between two parties that clearly specifies their mutual performance obligations. A performance contract has also been defined as a Memorandum of Understanding (MOU), rooted in the evaluation system, which comprehensively specifies the expected performance between the parties involved and holds each of the parties accountable to each other (Kobia& Huka, 2006). The main purpose is to ensure delivery of service in a transparent manner. Performance contracting has the same meaning as results-based management system—a term that has become very popular regarding performance of the public sectors in many African countries. Thus, public sector employees who sign performance contracts are required to justify their continued employment and pay based on positive evaluation of service outcomes delivered to their clients. Performance contracting should be looked at as a management tool currently being employed by most governments in developing countries to assist government policy makers in defining public service employees' responsibilities, rewards systems and expected performance.

The term performance contracting can be explained to have originated in France in the late 1970s, and other countries such India, Pakistan, and Korea have adopted performance contracting since (Organisation for Economic Co-operation and Development (OECD), 1997). In Africa, countries such as Nigeria, Gambia, Ghana, and Kenya have also adopted performance contracting as a strategy to optimize their human resources employed by the pubic sector (Kobia & Nura, 2006). The principal reason for the adoption of the performance contracting strategy in Africa was the fact that mere employment does not necessarily mean productivity (Nyamu, 2007). In many countries in Africa, the public service has been found to have many employees whose productivity has been found to be below the standards set. As Nyamu (2007), noted:

> the term employment has meant being hired at a salary and with a title to some undefined something supposed be performed in some room known as office, quite often enhanced with an official car and a driver. All these appendages to employment have militated against the spirit of service delivery to the intended clientele in favour of creating, quite unwittingly, big and small public service dictators too often unaware of their obligation to their employers. (p. 1)

Nyamu stated further that employment in the public service must, at all times, be associated with some kind of achievement. Without that achievement, it translates to squandering public (or corporate) resources, and must logically be terminated. Thus, contract performance is motivated by the idea that individual and organizational performance occurs when employment of individuals is strictly tied to results or concrete, visible, countable, demonstrable, and desirable outcomes and benefits accruing to the customers served by these individuals (Nyamu, 2007).

WHY PERFORMANCE CONTRACTS?

Across the world, the main rationales for implementing performance contracting include the following core reasons (Kobia & Nura, 2006, pp. 5–6):

1. Improve performance to deliver quality and timely services to citizens in the case of government departments and government-owned corporations.

2. Improve productivity in order to maximize the shareholders wealth in the case of public traded companies.
3. Reduce or eliminate reliance on the exchequer for recurrent and development expenditures by government-owned corporations.
4. Instill a sense of accountability and transparency in service delivery and in the utilization of the country's resources.
5. Give autonomy to government agencies without being subjected to the bureaucracies and unnecessary red tape which hampers efficient and effective delivery of goods and services to the customers.
6. Ensure that government owned agencies become competitive and profitable especially in this global and competitive environment.

From the six points above, one can persuasively argue that all government agencies in Africa need to implement performance contracts to remain viable through quality services to their customers. Performance contracts can play a major role in building customer loyalty based on customer satisfaction. The contracts hold all parties involved accountable.

GLOBAL TRENDS OF PERFORMANCE CONTRACTING

As noted earlier in this chapter, performance contracting in the public service started in France in the 1970s. The concept has taken a global dimension and is now being practiced in more than 30 developing countries. For instance, in Asia, performance contracting is now applied in Bangladesh, China, India, Malaysia, South Korea, Pakistan, and Sri Lanka. In Africa performance contracts have been implemented in both public and private enterprises in countries such as Benin, Burundi, Cameroon, Cape Verde, Congo, Cote d'Ivoire, Gabon, the Gambia, Ghana, Guinea, Madagascar, Mali, Mauritania, Morocco, Niger, Senegal, Togo, Tunisia, and Zaire. In South America, performance contracts are used in Argentina, Brazil, Bolivia, Chile, Colombia, Mexico, Uruguay, and Venezuela. In European countries such as the United Kingdom, the Netherlands, France, Italy, Denmark, and Finland, to mention a few, use performance contracts. In North America, the United States of America and Canada both use performance contracts.

PERFORMANCE CONTRACTS IN SELECTED AFRICAN COUNTRIES

Since this chapter's main focus is on performance contracting and the performance practices of African economies, this chapter provides selected case studies of the experience of some African countries with performance contracts as a strategy to improve human performance and productivity. According to the World Bank (2002), Ghana is one of the African countries which have successfully implemented performance contracts. In Ghana, beginning in 2000, the district assemblies and communities played a key role in planning for the supply of the water in the rural regions of the country. This new policy and structures attracted external funding. The World Bank (2002) noted further that the reform to implement performance contracts in Ghana began dialogue which involved major stakeholders including the general public communities and government officials. The dialogue resulted into a new rural water and sanitation policy. To ensure these policies' success, several large pilot projects from various parts of the country were implemented. The lessons learned from the pilot projects were incorporated into the national performance contract program aimed at ensuring project success. First, the national and international non-governmental organizations were contracted and involved in capacity building. The Community Water Supply Agency (CWSA) was created as a facilitating agency rather than an implementer. CWSA, as a semi-autonomous public-sector agency, signs an annual performance contract with the State Enterprise Commission. It is committed to staying efficient and lean (below 200 staff), and highly decentralized with its ten regional offices (World Bank, 2002).

The other country that has successfully implemented the use of performance contracts in African public service is Swaziland. The evolution of contract plans in Swaziland can be traced back to the early 1990s a period that witnessed the promulgation of the Public Enterprise (Control and Monitoring) Act of 1989 (Musa, 2001). The latter sought to establish viable control mechanisms for Swaziland's public sector amid a national outcry that public enterprises were continuing, unabated, to be a financial and administrative burden on the government (Musa, 2001). However, the performance contracts of the early 1990s failed to achieve their stated objective (i.e., to improve the performance of the public enterprises). This was because of widespread use of consultants in the formulation of contract plans, including the determination mechanisms for their monitoring and evaluation. Public enterprise management did not develop the necessary sense of ownership and commitment to the success of the enterprise contracts. Lessons of experience with regard to the use of outside consultants, experts or advisors, especially from developed countries, in the formulation of development plans in Africa, have shown that while they may be knowledgeable about certain issues and areas that are generic to their field of specialization, they often lack an intimate knowledge of the unique sociopolitical and economic circumstances confronting African countries (Musa, 2001).

In the Gambia, the performance contract system for public enterprises was introduced in 1987. As a prelude to identifying those Performance Enterprises to come under the performance contract system, the Public Enterprise sector was divided into three schedules: (1) Enterprises in which the government is a minority shareholder; (2) Enterprises in which the government is a majority shareholder or has 100% shareholding; and (3) Strategic corporation/departments.

Only Public Enterprises under schedule three were identified as suitable candidates for performance contracts. Under the first phase in 1987, the performance contracts were developed for three Public Enterprises only.

LESSON LEARNED FROM THE THREE AFRICAN COUNTRIES

As demonstrated above, the following lessons were learned from the implementation of performance contracts in Ghana, Swaziland and the Gambia: (1) to institutionalize and create ownership of the performance contract, public enterprise managers and citizens should be involved and let them manage the process rather than external expatriates with limited knowledge of the various economic, and sociopolitical dimensions of the African countries involved; (2) to recognize the great need for allocation of adequate resources to achieve the set target; (3) to select few realistic targets rather than too many objectives attempted at once; and (4) the government should honor their financial commitment to the enterprise.

PERFORMANCE CONTRACTING IN KENYA AS A STRATEGY FOR PERFORMANCE IMPROVEMENT IN THE PUBLIC SERVICE

In order to move the implementation of the results-based management (RBM) forward, the Government of Kenya developed and launched the Strategy for Performance Improvement in the Public Service in 2001. The Strategy sought to increase productivity and improve service by optimizing the human resources employed by the public service. It outlined the actions that were necessary to embed long lasting and sustainable change in the way public services are offered. Underpinning this strategy was the Results Oriented Management (ROM) approach, which makes it necessary to adjust operations to respond to predetermined objectives, outputs and results. The adoption of this approach demanded a paradigm shift in Government operations. This called for a transformation from a passive, inward-looking bureaucracy to one which was proactive, outward looking and results oriented; one that sought 'customer satisfaction' and 'value for money'. Consequently the ministries and all government departments were required to develop strategic plans which reflected their objectives derived from the 9th National Development Plan, the Poverty Reduction Strategy Paper and based on the Medium Term Expenditure Framework (MTEF), Sectoral Priorities and Millennium development Goals.

MANAGING FOR RESULTS IN KENYA'S PUBLIC SERVICE

According to the Government of Kenya, GOK, (2005a), introduction of Results-based Management (RBM) ensures that the public sector becomes more focused and responsive to the needs of those it serves. The result will be a sector directing its energies toward delivering targeted results for Kenyans and utilizing resources more productively. The quality and productivity of expenditures and investment will be improved to ensure cost-effectiveness and value-for-money. Results-based Management is about institutional as well as individual performance, both in quality and quantity (Nafukho, in press). The key elements of RBM are:

1. Performance target setting—the process of setting performance targets for ministries/departments, groups or individuals carrying out specific work assignments.
2. Performance planning—the process of establishing a shared understanding of what is to be achieved and how it is to be achieved and managing resources to ensure successful implementation.
3. Performance monitoring and reporting.
4. Performance appraisal—the process of evaluating organization, group or individual performance against predetermined targets.

The framework for managing results is at three levels namely: National, organizational (ministries and institutions) and individual. Embedded in the RBM framework are two key components to ensure its success, a performance management information system and a strong enforcement mechanism. The framework is a key part of government's commitment to improving the performance of public service delivery and is based on agreed national principals and values.

RESULT-BASED PERFORMANCE MANAGEMENT CYCLE

Figure 5.1 illustrates the performance management cycle and identifies performance contracting positions in the cycle.

In order to provide a mechanism that supports the achievement of Economic Recovery Strategy (ERS) and achievement of Millennium Develop-

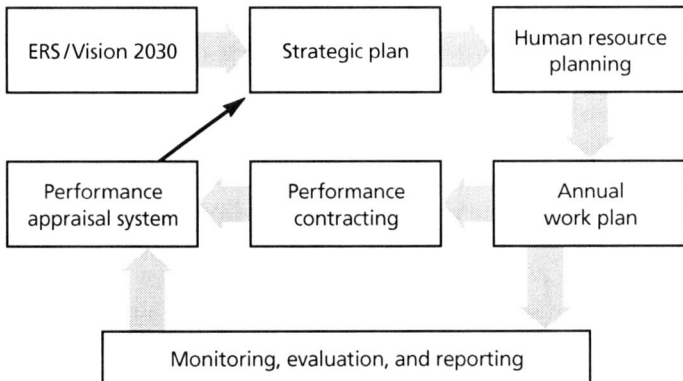

Figure 5.1 Performance management cycle. *Source:* Author's illustration

ment Goals (MDGs), all ministry and public enterprise must develop a Strategic Plan and strive to achieve its mission and objectives. Strategic planning in all public sector organizations should therefore aim at strengthening and looping linkages with policy, planning and budgeting. The human resource function needs to be aligned with the strategic goals of the organizations. Individuals derive individual work plans from the strategic plan. It is this work plan that forms a basis for the performance contract, which is then implemented, evaluated and the information used to inform decisions on performance improvement.

However, this process has not been without challenges. First, there is an absence of clear, well-formulated objectives based on a strategic plan. This makes it difficult to assess organizational and individual performance. Second, public enterprises develop strategic plans without involving all stakeholders, which leads to lack of ownership and in turn makes it difficult to achieve strategic objectives.

RATIONALE FOR REINTRODUCTION PERFORMANCE CONTRACTS

Performance Contracts in Kenya originated from the perception that the performance of the Public Sector has been consistently falling below the expectations of the Public. Performance Contracting is part of broader Public sector reforms aimed at improving efficiency and effectiveness in the management of Public service. The problems that have inhibited the performance of government agencies are common and have been identified as excessive controls, multiplicity of principles, frequent political interference, poor management, and outright mismanagement (Government of

Kenya, GOK, 2005a). While several approaches have been used to address these challenges, it is hoped that a performance contract will be an effective tool for managing productivity.

A Performance Contract is a freely negotiated performance agreement between government and the agency. It clearly specifies the intentions, obligations, responsibilities and powers of the parties. It addresses economic, social and other tasks to be discharged for Economic or other desired gain. The fundamental principle of performance contracting is the devolved management style where emphasis is management by outcome rather than management by processes. It therefore provides a framework for changing behaviors in the context of devolved management structures.

Governments all over the world view performance contracting as a useful vehicle for articulating clearer definitions of objectives and supporting new management monitoring and control methods, while at the same time leaving day-to-day management to the managers themselves. It organizes and defines tasks so management can perform them systematically, purposefully and with reasonable probability of achievement. Performance Contracts are based on the premise that what gets measured gets done; if you cannot see and measure success, you cannot reward it; if you cannot recognize failure, you cannot correct it and if you can demonstrate results, you can win public support. The Government has adopted Performance Contracting in the Public Service in order to ensure that:

1. There is reduction or altogether elimination of reliance on exchequer funding for government agencies which are expected to generate revenue or make profit.
2. An objective basis for divesting loss making government agencies, it will also compel the agencies to give a return to the shareholders by paying dividends or surplus.
3. The process will ensure that government ministries/departments improve service delivery to the public.

GENESIS OF PERFORMANCE CONTRACTING IN KENYA

The concept of performance Contracting was first introduced in the management of state corporations in 1989. A Parastatal Reform Strategy Paper, which was approved by cabinet in 1991, was the first official recognition of the concept of Performance Contracting as it was part of the following policies that were recommended to streamline and improve the performance of State Corporations (Masai & Mulei, 2005, p. 197).

1. Divestiture or Liquidation of non-strategic government corporations.

2. Contracting out Commercial activities to the private sector.
3. Permitting private sector competition for existing state monopolies.
4. Improvements in the enabling environment of all strategic government corporations including removal of potentially conflicting objectives. Performance Contracts, where applicable will be used to make transparent the cost of social services and to compensate the corporations for their net costs.

The first two government corporations to be on Performance Contracting were Kenya Railways Corporation and the National Cereals and Produce Board. Kenya Railways signed PC's in April 1989 and National Cereals and Produce Board signed in November 1990.

THE OBJECTIVES OF INTRODUCING PERFORMANCE CONTRACTS IN KENYA

1. Improve service delivery to the public by ensuring that top-level managers are accountable for results.
2. Reversing the decline in efficiency and ensuring that resources are focused on attainment of Key national policy priorities of the government (Parachuted projects).
3. Institutionalizing performance oriented culture in the public Service through introduction of an objective performance appraisal system.
4. Measure and Evaluate Performance.
5. Linking reward to measurable performance.
6. Facilitate the attainment of desired results.
7. Instill accountability for results at the highest level in the government.
8. Ensure that the culture of accountability pervades all levels of the government machinery.
9. Strengthen and clarify the obligation required of the government and its employees in order to achieve agreed target. (Government of Kenya, GOK, 2005b, p. 4)

OUTCOME OF THE TWO PERFORMANCE CONTRACTS

The implementation of Performance Contracts by the Kenya Railways Corporation and the National Cereals and Produce Board eventually failed due to the following reasons:

1. Lack of Political goodwill to drive this process. It was perceived as donor-driven.
2. The performance contracts did not conform to the requirements of the three subsystems of performance contracts lacked the performance incentive system.
3. There was no provision for the impact of external factors such as changes in Kenya government's policy, inflation, exchange rate fluctuations that would have made evaluation fair. (Government of Kenya, GOK, 2005b, p. 7)

REINTRODUCTION OF PERFORMANCE CONTRACTING

The Government of Kenya decided to reintroduce performance contracting in 2003. The initiative to introduce performance contracts in Kenya came from President Mwai Kibaki and was clearly spelt out in the Economic Recovery Strategy for Wealth and Employment Creation (ERSWEC).

In August 2003, the government appointed a committee to spearhead the introduction and implementation of Performance Contracts, namely the performance Contracts Steering Committee. The government made a decision to introduce PC in state corporations on a pilot basis in 2004. Sixteen State Corporations signed the PC's by December 2004. The criteria for selecting the pilot companies included representation of diverse sectors and corporations with Strategic plans. Following the success in implementing performance contracts in state corporations, the government extended the process to Public Service beginning with Permanent Secretaries and accounting officers. Further, in April 2005, Government decided to place the management of 175 Local Authorities on Performance Contracts (African Association for Public Administration and Management, 2005).

Accordingly, five major municipalities completed Performance Contracts on 30th September 2005 on pilot basis; these are:

1. City Council of Nairobi.
2. Mombasa Municipal Council.
3. Eldoret Municipal Council.
4. Kisumu Municipal Council.
5. Nakuru Municipal Council.

EXPECTED OUTCOME OF PERFORMANCE CONTRACTS IN KENYA

The expected outcomes of performance contracts in Kenya are listed below:

1. Improved performance.
2. Decline in reliance on exchequer funding.
3. Increased transparency in operations and resource utilization.
4. Increased accountability for results.
5. Linking reward on measurable performance.
6. Reduced confusion resulting from Multiplicity of objectives.
7. Clear apportionment of responsibility for action.
8. Improvement in the correlation between planning and implementation.
9. Creating a fair and accurate impression on the performance.
10. Greater autonomy.
11. Creation of enabling legal and regulatory environment.

IMPACTS OF PERFORMANCE CONTRACTING IN KENYA

While performance contracts have been used in many countries of the world, in Africa, the adoption and use of performance contracts have been done with many objections from the employees involved. For instance, in Kenya's seven public universities, the vice chancellors were among the first public service employees to sign five year performance contracts. When the time came for the lecturers to sign the performance contracts, the University Academic Staff Union (UASU) objected. Currently, public university lecturers in Kenya do not have to sign performance contracts like their counterparts in other parts of the world. When the Teachers' Service Commission (TSC), a government organization responsible for the employment of teachers serving in public schools wanted to introduce performance contracts in 2007, the Kenya National Union of Teachers (KNUT), objected and the decision was shelved. "When the Kenya National Union of Teachers declares publicly that it will not accept the publicly acclaimed performance contracting strategy, many professionals are baffled as to whether the teaching fraternity appreciates the seriousness of their open confrontation with public policy declarations (Nyamu, 2007). The implementation of the Process of Performance Contracting began in 2004 and was faced with several difficulties such as the resentment by the Unions, and the unwillingness of civil service employees to sign performance contracts. The real impact of the process is yet to be fully visible. However, there is clear evidence of radical improvement particularly in the following aspects of the management of Public Service:

1. Remarkable and unprecedented improvement in profit generation for commercial state corporations.
2. Significant improvement in service delivery and operations by such ministries as immigrations and registration of Persons, Agriculture,

Provincial Administration and Internal Security, Health, finance and Water.
3. Significant improvement in operations and services by Nairobi City Council, Kisumu and Nakuru Municipalities.
4. Unprecedented improvement in service delivery and operations by the bulk of state corporations and statutory boards, among them, KenGen, Kenya Power and Lighting Company Limited, Kenya Ports Authority, Kenya Utalii College, National Oil Corporation of Kenya, Kenyatta International Conference Centre, etc.

EMPIRICAL EVIDENCE OF THE IMPACT OF PERFORMANCE CONTRACTS IN KENYA

To understand the successes and challenges of implementing performance contracting in Kenya, a survey was carried out among the civil servants. A questionnaire was developed from performance contract literature and administered to a purposeful sample identified during training. The results presented in this chapter are based on primary data collected from a sample of 280 senior public service course participants at Kenya Institute of Administration (K.I.A.). Data were collected from the course participants who were central in the implementation of performance contract in the ministries.

DEMOGRAPHIC CHARACTERISTICS OF THE RESPONDENTS

Data were collected from the participants of a senior management course, and performance appraisal system course. The demographic information sought were on gender, age, education level, marital status, number of years in the civil service, job group on first appointment, current job group, and number of years in the job group and the name of the ministry assigned. Highlights of the characteristics are presented in Table 5.1.

CHARACTERISTICS OF THE RESPONDENTS

Two hundred and thirty-one males and forty-nine females who had attended the senior management course and performance Appraisal system at KIA were surveyed. Male participants represented 82.5% of the respondents. The ages of the respondents ranged from 35 to over fifty. Regarding marital status, 22 (7.9) were single, 256 (91.4) were married while 2 (0.7%) were divorced. Concerning their level of education, 101(36%) had a diploma, 130 (46%) had a bachelors degree while 44 had a Master's degree. Majority

TABLE 5.1 Demographic Characteristics of the Respondents

Characteristic	*n*	Percent
Gender		
Male	231	82.5
Female	49	17.5
Age		
Below 35	25	8.9
35–40	92	32.9
41–45	79	28.2
46–50	52	18.6
50 and above	32	11.4
Marital status		
Single	22	7.9
Married	256	91.4
Divorced	2	0.7
Level of education		
Diploma	101	36.1
Bachelors	130	46.4
Masters	44	15.7
PhD	3	1.1
When joined service		
Before 1986	101	36.1
1987–1992	83	29.6
1993–1998	80	28.6
1999–2002	4	1.4
2003–2006	9	3.2
Number of years in JG		
Less than 1 year	21	7.5
1–3 years	131	46.8
4–6 years	66	23.6
7–9 years	27	9.6
above 10 years	31	11.1
Current work station		
Coast	13	4.6
Nairobi	146	52.1
Nyaza	19	6.8
North Eastern	4	1.4
Central	23	8.2
Eastern	26	9.3
Western	16	5.7
Rift Valley	26	9.3
Ministries participating		
Ministry of Finance	60	21.4
Office of the president	58	20.7
Ministry of labour HD	53	18.9
Ministry of Roads	24	8.6
Office of VP	22	7.9
Ministry of LFDev	20	7.1
Others	41	12.0

of the respondents 131(46.8) had been in their current job group for three years while 66 (23%) had been in the same job group between 4–6 years. While all the provinces of Kenya were represented in the group, majority of the respondent's workstation was in Nairobi. Ministries that had a higher number representation in the survey were Finance with 60 (21.4%), Office of the President 58 (20.7%), and Ministry of Labor (18.9%).

UNDERSTANDING OF PERFORMANCE CONTRACT

To investigate if the participants knew the goal of performance contracting, the participants were required to state the goal of performance contracting in their ministries. A majority of the respondents, 205 (72.2%) summed the goal as to improve performance/enhance efficiency and effectiveness in service delivery through a transparent and accountable manner. Further, 206 (73.6%) said their ministries had signed the second (2006/7) performance contract with the Government. The responses indicated that majority of the participants were conversant with performance contract.

The Strategic plan is a critical management tool in performance contracting. The participants were asked whether their ministries had developed strategic plans. Of these participants, 242 (86.4%) indicated that their ministry had strategic plans, while 31(11.1%) indicated that they did not have. Closely related to a strategic plan is the departmental work plan aligned with performance contract. A majority of the respondents 223 (79.6%) indicated that they had departmental work plan, while 43 (15.4%) did not. In addition, slightly over half of the respondents 159 (56%) indicated that they had developed individual work plan in line with their ministry performance contract.

A service charter is an agreement of what the organization promises to do to satisfy their customers. A majority of the respondents, 187, (66.8 %) said that their ministries had developed service charters. However only 88 (31.4 %) were involved in the development of their Ministry's service charter. Regarding training in performance contracting, only 57 respondents said they had received training in performance contracting while a majority, 212, (75.5%) had not received any. It is interesting to note that 208 participants (74.3%) said they would require further training on all aspect of performance contracting.

ATTITUDES TOWARD IMPLEMENTATION
OF PERFORMANCE CONTRACTS

A majority of the respondents (179 or 63.9%) felt that the performance contract had helped improve communication with the public while 164 (68.6%) agreed that performance contract would increase accountability among public officers. An overwhelming majority (217 or 77.5%) of the respondents felt that performance contracts had introduced setting of the individual job expectations and staff performance plans. More than 166 participants felt that as a result of performance contract, performance targets are fairly distributed in their departments. A majority, 205, (74.2%) of the respondents indicated that with the introduction of performance contract, public servants are increasingly seeking to multi-skill and diversify to remain on the job.

More than 60% of the respondents indicated that, with the implementation of performance of contracts, public servants are more involved in decision making, felt evaluation of the performance is done fairly, that they knew where to seek assistance concerning meeting the targets, and that implantation has assisted in understanding government policy documents. However, 174 (62.1%) respondents indicated that they do not have sufficient resources to meet their targets. Table 5.2 shows that with the introduction of performance contract, the participants were generally enjoying their jobs.

TABLE 5.2   After Introduction of the Performance Contract, What Was the Quality of Their Work Most of the Time?

Response on their work most of the time was:	*n*	Percent
Satisfying	156	55.7
Creative	155	55.4
Challenging	186	66.4
Interesting	149	53.2
Feel more responsible	162	57.9
Sense of accomplishment	156	56.4
Performance is better	219	75.7

Results from the above analysis indicate that the participant's views regarding performance contracting are positive and support the objectives of performance contracting objectives. In other words, performance contract is enhancing job satisfaction for the participants; hopefully their satisfaction would lead to improved job performance.

CHALLENGES OF IMPLEMENTING PERFORMANCE CONTRACTING IN KENYA

To investigate participants' experience with the implementation of performance contract, several questions were asked regarding whether the participants had signed performance contracts with their supervisor and whether they had experienced any problems with implementation of the performance contract. It was interesting to find out only 25 out of the 280 participants had signed the performance contract. Some of the problems experienced during the implementation of the performance contract include lack of adequate resources, resources not being released on time; some performance targets were highly ambitious and unplanned transfer of staff.

Respondents went ahead to suggest ways of ensuring performance contract is successful in their workplace. Some of the suggestions given by a significant (more than 30) number of participants include continuous training on PC, allocation of adequate resources; development of a reward system for performers, increased salaries, enhanced teamwork and available resources on time in that order.

LESSONS LEARNED AND RECOMMENDATIONS

In general, performance contracting has induced the public service to become more oriented toward customers, markets and performance, without putting the provision of essential public services into jeopardy. The introduction of contracts and management by results is used to increase the performance as it emphasizes better the human resource management. Performance management strategies pursue three objectives namely, saving, internal management improvement and better accountability (OECD, 1997). Some of the lessons drawn from the Kenyans experiences, as well as from the review of literature, include:

1. A solid legal framework, which sets out the basic premises and the status of the contract, may avoid ad hoc and fragmented solutions. The current arrangements lack enforcement legal capacities. Sanctions can be questioned as in the case of the seven senior officers

from Kenya Revenue Authority who are seeking legal redress after jobs were terminated as a result of not meeting their performance targets.

2. Stability of resources enhances the motivating effect of the contract. When resources are not available or arrived late, the staff gets frustrated. The majority of respondents in the public service expressed this view.

3. The political top must respect the operational autonomy of the contracted organizations/ministries. Knowledge of strategic planning, development of work plans and monitoring capacities among the staff is central to the success of PC and the management support and their technical knowledge is crucial.

4. Contract management should be accompanied by performance-oriented change in the public service structure and management culture. Culture that empowers staff to embrace and manage change is necessary. Management instruments, focusing on performance and cost in the field of human resources and financial management should be developed in an integrated manner.

5. There needs to be a good definition of outputs and solid performance measures. This requires a well-defined training program for the public servants to support implementation.

6. Other instruments of control (such as quality service charters and regulations concerning transparency and accountability) must complement performance contracting. PC tends to emphasize competition among staff to meet their targets. Competition if not well controlled may bring conflicts with values hence interfere with organization culture.

7. Performance contracting is not a cure for poor management. PC will only succeed where best management practices are practiced. Top management key competencies and participatory approach to decision making is crucial.

8. There should be regular overall evaluations and audits of benefits and drawbacks of the implemented contract in order to learn from experiences. Differences in implementing contexts may provide different learning experiences. For example, Canadian experience may not fully work very well in some African countries hence the need to consider the regional context.

9. The early years of implementing PC are difficult both for the staff and management. A degree of tolerance from the management may sustain the momentum. Mistakes are likely to be made but what is critical is drawing lessons for innovations and creativity for future performance improvements.

RECOMMENDATIONS FOR FURTHER RESEARCH

To further understand the implementation of PC in Kenya, the chapter suggests areas of further research that may provide more insights on the successes and challenges and lessons learned such as:

1. Future research should focus on the role of Results Office in the implementation of PC in Kenya. Such investigations would reveal the strength of the secretariat in leading the implementation of PC in all the ministries.
2. A comparative study to investigate the extent to which State Corporations and the Ministries are in implementing the PC in Kenya. Comparing the differences in the successes or failure in State corporation and Ministries would be an interesting area to explore to gain insights into factors that enhance or inhibit the implementation of PC in Kenya.
3. Future research study focusing on larger sample public servants perceptions on the role of PC in improving service delivery is needed. There is a relationship between perceptions and behavior.
4. Further research effort is needed to establish if Kenyan citizens perceive service delivery has been improved since the implementation of PC in Kenya. Results of such a study would confirm if the objectives of implementing PC are being achieved in Kenya.
5. Finally, future research should deal with assessment of legal and regulatory environment to find out the extent to which they facilitate or inhibit implementation of PC in Kenya.

CONCLUSION

The Kenya government's commitment to the provision of effective, efficient and ethical services for social economic development continues to be the driving force behind many initiatives that have recently been introduced into the public service. Although there have been several initiatives since 1993, Performance Contract was implemented in Kenya in 2003. This was a Government attempt to provide a unifying framework within which performance can be managed in the public service to achieve the goals outlined in the Economic Recovery Strategy.

This chapter has defined performance and explained the meaning of performance improvement. In addition, the chapter has traced the origin of performance contracts and their relevance to various governments of the world. Specific case studies of how performance contracts have been applied in Africa, specifically Kenya, are discussed. The chapter further highlights the three phases of public sector reforms in Kenya and identifies the fit of performance contract as a management tool within the third phase of the wider public sector reforms. The definitions of performance contract as well as the success and challenges and lessons learned in the implementation of PC in Kenya are discussed. The empirical results from a purposeful sample of 280 training participants show the perceived successes, challenges and suggestions for Implementing PC in Kenya. Further, the chapter makes recommendations regarding the need for research to guide the successful implementation and management of performance contracts in Kenya and in other African countries.

REFERENCES

African Association for Public Administration and Management (AAPAM). (2005). The enabling state and the role of the public service in wealth creation: Problems and strategies for development in Africa. *The report of the 26th Roundtable Conference of the African Association for Public Administration and Management.* Mombassa, Kenya: Government Printer.

Gilbert, T. F. (1978). *Human competence: Engineering worthy performance.* New York: McGraw-Hill.

Gilbert, T. F. (1988). Measuring the potential for performance improvement. *Training, 25*(7), 49–52.

Gilbert, T. F. (1996). *Human competence: Engineering worthy performance* (2nd ed.). Washington, DC: International Society for Performance Improvement.

Government of Kenya (GOK). (2005a). RBM Guide, Kenya. *Results based management: Training manual.* Nairobi: Government Printer.

Government of Kenya (GOK). (2005b). *Sensitization and training manual on performance contracts in the public service.* Nairobi: Government Printer.

Government of Kenya (GOK). (2003). *Economic recovery strategy for wealth and employment creation.* Nairobi: Government Printer.

Government of Kenya (GOK). (2001). *A strategy for performance improvement in the public service.* Nairobi: Government Printer.

Gradous, D. B. (1989). *Systems theory applied to human resource development.* Alexandria, VA: American Society for Training and Development.

Holton, E. F. III (1999). Performance domains and their boundaries. *Advances in Developing Human Resources, 1,* 26–46.

Kobia, M., & Huka N. M. (2006). The Kenyan experience with performance contracting. Paper presented during the *African Association for Public Administration and Management Conference* on the theme: Towards an effective delivery of public services in Africa. Arusha, Tanzania, December 4–8.

Masai W. S. & Mullei A. K. (2005). *Improving financial sector performance in Kenya.* Nairobi, Kenya. Government Printer.

Musa, P. D. (2001). *Contract plans and public enterprise performance: The case of Swaziland.* Tangier, Morocco: African Training and Research Center in Administra-

tion for Development. Retrieved January 8, 2008, from: http: http://unpan1.
un.org/intradoc/groups/public/documents/CAFRAD/UNPAN005260.pdf.

Nafukho, F. M. (in press). Consensus building, dialogue and spirituality principles
of the learning organization paradigm: Implications for Kenya's public service reform agenda. *Journal of Third World Studies.*

Nyamu, H. (2007). *Teachers union got it all wrong on performance contracts.* Retrieved January 6, 2008, from: http://www.zibb.com/301.aspx?a=1703679&h=Teachers
+Union+Got+It+All+Wrong+On+Performance+Contracts+%5bopinion%5d.

Organisation for Economic Co-operation and Development (OECD). (1997). *In
search of results: Performance management practices.* Paris: Author.

Rotter, J. B. (1982). *The development and application of social learning theory.* New York:
Praeger.

Rummler, G. A., & Brache, A. P. (1995). *Improving performance: How to manage the
white space on the organization chart* (2nd ed.). San Francisco: Jossey-Bass Publishers.

Steinmetz, L. L., & Todd, R. H. Jr. (1992). *First-line management: Approaching supervision effectively* (5th ed.). Homewood, IL: Irwin.

Swanson, R. A. (1999). The foundations of performance improvement and implications for practice. *Advances in Developing Human Resources, 1,* 1–25.

Swanson, R. A., & Arnold, D. E. (1997). The purpose of HRD is to improve performance. In R. Rowden (Ed.), *Workplace learning: Debating five critical questions of
theory and practice* (pp. 13–19). San Francisco: Jossey-Bass.

Vroom, V. H. (1964). *Work and motivation.* New York: Wiley.

Weinberger, L. A. (1998). Commonly held theories of human resource development. *Human Resource Development International, 1*(1), 75–93.

World Bank (2002). *Public enterprises in Sub Saharan Africa.* Washington DC: Author.

Yamnill, S., & McLean, G. N. (2001). Theories supporting transfer of training. *Human Resource Development Quarterly, 12*(2), 195–208.

CHAPTER 6

EXAMINING HUMAN PERFORMANCE IN SOUTH AMERICA

Jules K. Beck

To analyze human performance in a Latin context, one must consider the forces for change that have impacted development in South America for decades. Political, economic, and grassroots movements have typically generated complex social conditions that have either supported capacity building among populations or constrained that development. This chapter of Human Performance Models Revealed in the Global Contexts focuses on South American institutions, organizations, and movements that are building capacity to improve the welfare of impoverished populations by ameliorating conditions that prevent people from contributing fully to themselves, their families, and their communities, or by supporting grassroots development activities that help individuals and communities actualize their potential for self-support and growth.

While the major focus of this chapter is on what individuals and communities have done to further their own sustenance through grassroots development efforts, the larger issues of global trade, government, and economic free-market reforms are also considered. The potential for increasing human performance depends in many ways on the economic and political systems which define the environment. Hence, we first examine those technical, systemic elements to see how the gaps in systems comprise an

Human Performance Models Revealed in the Global Context, pages 103–127
Copyright © 2009 by Information Age Publishing

important facet among many variables that impact the potential for growth in human performance (USAID Office of Population, n.d.).

INTRODUCTION

Competing interests have often created paradoxes in Latin America. As education has become more available to average citizens—according to Hurtado (2006), 70% of the Chilean university population "are the first members of their families to reach this educational level" (p. 5) since increased contemporary education may not necessarily support society's long-term interest. Stromquist (2002, p. 157) describes a link between higher education that increasingly satisfies the demands of economic production through greater flexibility and availability, that nonetheless might narrow "what is considered knowledge worth learning, the weakening of the social perception of education as a public good." She adds that the entrepreneurial focus becomes one of "profit and narrowly defined knowledge, rather than a "broader humanistic understanding."

Another paradox arises when one considers the demands on natural resources experienced in third world countries. Greater global consumption has affected South America, from the rich, cattle-laden pampas of Argentina and the Amazonian soils of Brazil, to the oil fields of Venezuela, industrialized countries have often reaped the benefits of developing countries' natural resources while at the same time depleting those resources in an uneven exchange. The reaping of those benefits, however, might contribute to a deteriorating environment that has implications for social justice, as Stromquist (2002) notes, where "the great share of those who face the negative ecological consequences are the poor" and who might even be subject to loss of "indigenous lands and rights" (p. 158).

Another example of a paradox can be found in Venezuela, where the state has recently increased control over its oil industry, which prior to the new government was a fairly autonomous operation under the previous administration. Under the Chavez regime, private producers have been confronted with new, restrictive policies or nationalization of their interests. Terry Karl (2007) from Stanford University described the negative consequences of a wealth-generating industry in a developing country (in Rosenberg, 2007, p. 44):

> Oil not only creates very few jobs, it also destroys jobs in other sectors. By pushing up a country's exchange rate, the export of oil distorts the economy. Oil [drives] out any other productive activity... [why] bother to produce your own food if you could buy it? Why... bother to develop any kind of export industry if oil makes your money worth more and that hurts all your other exports?

Rosenberg (2007) agrees with Karl, noting that countries that are dependent on oil or gas have been generally ill-governed, and "with one or two exceptions...are poorer, more-conflict ridden and despotic." Further, she characterizes Venezuela as "a typical victim of the oil curse. It has become a rich country of poor people" (p. 44).

The following sections build upon these observations of paradox to examine some consequences of trade policy and income distribution, trade agreements, free-market effects, and political alliances. The last sections present selected in-depth examples of non-governmental organizations (NGOs) and grassroots activities that have focused on building sustainable capacity for individuals and their communities.

TRADE POLICY AND INCOME DISTRIBUTION

Debt-ridden Latin American countries faced financial crises beginning in the mid-1970s (Berry, 1997). A process of "poverty alleviation" had been underway in most of Latin America through the 1960s and early 1970s. During this time, where a "growth without redistribution" appeared to be the norm, "within a context of an essentially unchanged and steep level of income inequality," that nonetheless, outpaced other third world countries since the average Latin American income exceeded theirs (Berry, 1997, pp. 3–4).

In response to the crises, the international financial community, through multilateral organizations such as the International Monetary Fund (IMF), forced many Latin American countries to adopt a structural process of economic reform that relied on liberalizing, market-friendly strategies (Berry, 1997; Devlin & Vodusek, 2005; Molyneux, 2002). Stromquist (2002) claims that transnational organizations (TNCs) "can force cuts in public expenditure and devaluation of currencies; it can diminish with great ease governments' expenditures on welfare policies" (p. 159). That "neo-liberalism" approach generally included export-led growth, the lowering of barriers to trade, such as tariffs, inviting greater foreign investment, the loosening of labor rules, extensive privatization, enhancing intellectual property rights, and other strategies to deregulate economies. An overarching result was that the state was now expected to take a much smaller role in the economic well-being of its citizenry.

The growth of global trade has forced many third-world countries to create strategies to increase their participation in the burgeoning global economy. Devlin and Vodusek (2005) characterize this requirement as a new circumstance for many countries where "the demand to intensify an insertion into the world economy often advances faster than their institutional capacities to formulate effective strategies, trade policies, and institutions" (p. 1).

According to Berry (1997), Latin American countries that introduced market-friendly economic reforms suffered serious increases in inequality. He notes that "the only countries that did not suffer a net decline in gross national income per capita between 1980 and 1992 were Colombia and Chile" (p. 5). Berry adds that there is "accumulating evidence that market-friendly policy shifts have been systematically associated with an abrupt and significant deterioration in income distribution" (p. 7).

How does Berry (1997, p. 9) reconcile the contradiction between the classic economic theory "that freeing of trade should shift...demand in favor of unskilled labor and agriculture and thereby improve the distribution of income" and the popular view that "freer markets generally increase inequality," mainly due to the abundance of labor in developing countries that compromise the economic welfare of unskilled workers in developed countries? Berry suggests a compelling argument for the latter:

> where activities shift from the source country to the host country when the capital flows from the former to the latter are less capital- and skill-intensive than the average in the source country, but more capital- and skill-intensive than the average in the host country. As a result, the capital and skilled-labor share of income rises in both countries. (p. 9)

Barry (1997) further buttresses his argument that TNCs dominate due to the economy of scale they provide international trade in the areas of product and finance. He adds that, for industrial countries, labor regulation—such as union recognition or minimum wages—usually narrows "earnings differentials, either by preventing the exploitation of relatively undefended workers or by preventing differences in ability from being reflected in earnings levels" (p. 10). That protection, however, "increases the inequality of labor income because its coverage is typically limited to a small labor elite" (p. 10).

Molyneux (2002) viewed the structural economic reforms as causing a rise in criminal activity and "deterioration of the social fabric" that led to political forces both on the left and the right calling for new development policies to offset the negative effects of restructuring. They proposed a new objective of restoring "the fabric of society through activating greater participation, more community level networks and ties of social solidarity" (p. 173). The World Bank in its 1997 Report called for "greater efforts to take the burden off the state by involvement of citizens and communities in the delivery of core collective goods." According to the president of the World Bank, "Participation matters—not only as a means of improving development effectiveness...but as the key to long-term sustainability and leverage" (p. 175).

Ultimately, the envisioned restoration of the social fabric would have to involve a new democratization process that would differ according to an individual country's political institutions, laws, infrastructure, and cultural context. While trade might open states to a larger economic arena, free-market policies that increased the wealth of nations but impoverished selected populations would require other, offsetting strategies to economically empower individuals and their communities.

TRADE AGREEMENTS

Trade Related Capacity Building (TRCB) represents a commitment to opening national borders to strategies to create opportunity for economic growth beneficial to all levels of a society. Where third-world countries employed high tariffs to discourage the flight of national capital, they were unlikely to develop the institutions and infrastructure needed to support free-market, competitive trade. Those economic preconditions are needed to attract foreign investment as well as local investment to streamline current operations and manufacturing systems as well as fund educational and technological changes supportive to furthering trade.

As Devlin and Vodusek (2005) report, "one of the strategic objectives of trade is to improve articulation with the world economy. The broad rationale behind this approach is to capture the opportunities for growth and transformation that more open economies offer" (p. 3).

One means to accomplish this objective is to do so either through unilateral activity, or through multilateral agreement with one's neighbors or significant trading partners. The Andean Pact was founded in 1969 by Bolivia, Chile, Colombia, Ecuador and Peru. The pact transformed into the Andean Community in the 1990s, with some change of membership until 2006, when the trading group reverted to its original members, minus Chile (Andean Community, 2006).

Other multilateral alliances came to fruition beginning in the early 1990s, culminating in the current agreements with MERCOSUR (referred to as "the Southern Cone"). The Andean Community gained four Associate Members in Argentina, Brazil, Paraguay and Uruguay. Argentina, Brazil, Paraguay and Uruguay were founding members of MERCOSUR in 1991 (European Union, n.d., para. 1).

A number of bilateral and multilateral free trade agreements (FTAs) were listed by Devlin and Vodusek (2005) as starting in the 1990s: Southern Cone-Common Market (1991), Chile-MERCOSUR (1996), Bolivia-MERCOSUR (1997), Bolivia-Mexico (1995), Chile-Peru (1998), Chile-Mexico (1999), Central America-Chile (2002), Chile-South Korea (2003), Canada-Chile (1997), Chile-US (2003), and Chile-EU (2003).

Devlin and Vodusek (2005) described the pros and cons of trade where it had not been viewed as a development tool and where most activities took place with other Latin countries:

> Trade agreements can generate net social welfare gains, but inevitably also create losers as well as winners. Part of the net gains must be used to compensate vulnerable groups, especially those who are already poor. This is based on equity considerations but also political economy as losing sectors will be more disposed to oppose integration if they anticipate that they will be left unprotected. (p. 14)

The market-friendly economic forces at work may open opportunities for workers, provided they can acquire the skills needed to move to industries that have become more competitive globally. They would have to overcome barriers of age, the need to relocate, or lack of training opportunities. Devlin and Vodusek also note that "rural sectors producing domestic staples may be especially vulnerable" (p. 14).

In a larger reality, individual countries must be responsible for building the infrastructure that will enable their populations to get the education they need, the health care that will help them remain on the job, and the ability to reach areas of greater economic activity by "improving roads, railroads, and ports" while they "attract national and foreign capital" (Devlin & Vodusek, 2005, p. 14).

In summary, TRCB can bring great opportunities for South American countries to increase economic activity for all citizens, provided institutions and policies are developed that can be tailored to meet similar development needs across partnering borders.

LIBERALIZING MARKETS IN SOUTH AMERICA

It is instructive to consider how the demands of free-market economic reforms initially affected South American countries. Depending on the existing political context, countries responded to international economic conditions in different ways. The following examples illustrate the impact of countries' adoption of the liberalizing structural changes of lowering trade barriers, relaxing labor regulation, and changing other internal institutions to meet the demands of the new financial reforms.

Argentina

Argentina, like the other Southern Cone members, adopted liberalizing market reforms in the early to mid-1970s, prior to most of the remaining

Latin American countries. Hence, it was possible to measure the effects of the new policies over a longer period of time (Berry, 1997). Barry notes that Argentina "suffered unusual worsening of income distribution" and "falling labor incomes for the lower deciles" (p. 12).

Bolivia

After successfully renegotiating its international debt, in 2000 Bolivia secured funding from the Inter-American Foundation, the United Nations Development Program, and the Inti Raymi Foundation to address the pervasive poverty in both urban and rural communities. The government sponsored a series of meetings, with the objective of developing institutional reforms to be focused on education and health issues (Krueger, 2002). Instead, "Bolivians looked for recognition and promotion of the small-scale activities that offer a livelihood to the poor and that generate the overwhelming majority of jobs, goods and services that make up the Bolivian economy" (p. 40). Representatives of poor communities called for building capacity through entrepreneurial ventures that would support the poor through "micro-enterprises, artisan workshops, rural businesses and mining cooperatives" (p. 40).

Chile

Under the Pinochet regime, the extensive privatization of state-enterprises during a severe recession led to a concentration of ownership and the formation of large conglomerates. During this time a concentration in land ownership developed at the expense of small farmers. Even more devastating to civil society was the reform of labor legislation that:

> relaxed regulations on dismissing workers, suspended unions until 1979, greatly reduced the social security tax paid by employers, and reduced other non-wage costs as well. After the second crisis (1981–1983), wage indexation was abolished and replaced by a real-wage "floor."...Taxes on wealth and capital gains were eliminated, profit tax rates substantially reduced, private banks and other debtors bailed out with public funds, and public employment greatly curtailed. Unemployment rates [rose up] to 25 percent. (Berry, 1997, pp. 13–16)

Berry (2007) also describes another contributor to income inequality as "an increase in the relative income of persons with university education vis-à-vis those with less schooling" (p. 16). By 1992, the unemployment rate in Chile had declined to 5%.

Hurtado (2006) describes some positive results of Chile's reforms. He agrees that the most important reform in education was aimed to improve equitable access and quality at all levels. Another advance in equity was anticipated in 2000 when a new unemployment insurance scheme was created; however it "does not cover workers with unstable or informal employments, which constitute the majority of the jobs of the poor" (p. 11).

Hurtado (2006) also considers the pension system as the most important pending social reform to increase equity in Chile. This pension system is based "on individual private accounts and thus reproduces the existing inequities in the labor market and excludes workers with no labor contract...coverage [remains] the highest in Latin America" (p. 11). He notes that unprotected workers are mostly poor and mostly women having no or few qualifications for employment.

Colombia

Colombia's experience with free-market reforms was markedly different from most of the Latin American countries. Colombia has changed its economic policies to accommodate the new liberalized model without the urgency of an economic crisis (Berry, 2007). Its labor-market reforms occurred mostly in the early 1990s, while "income distribution in three of Colombia's largest four cities revealed a significant lessening in inequality [of income distribution]" (p. 25). Of greater concern, however, was that although urban incomes rose substantially (by 18 percent over a three-year period), rural incomes fell "by at least 5 percent...probably due to production problems in the agricultural sector...and the price impact of the [liberalization policies]" (p. 25).

Ecuador

Ecuador became an oil exporter during the 1970s and went through a period of rapid economic growth as a result (Berry, 1997). Export earnings were used to modernize both industry and agriculture; however, extensive borrowing from abroad fueled continued growth after oil exports stagnated toward the end of the 1970s (Berry, 1997). From 1980 to 1993, exports grew by 6.3 percent; although "trade worsened by 36 percent in the same period, while prices for oil, coffee, and cacao all plummeted" (p. 27). By 1990, import tariffs had been reduced and import restrictions lifted resulting in a dramatic increase in the importation of consumer goods. Meanwhile, the liberalization of labor policies led to declining minimum wages even as it increased the flexibility preferred by foreign investors (Berry, 1997).

Uruguay

Uruguay's shift to a free-market economy paralleled that of its Southern Cone neighbors. Its introduction to liberalization reforms also began in the early 1970s, resulting from a continuing period of stagnation and high inflation (Berry, 1997). A new military government introduced freer import licensing and labor requirements, abolished import licensing and quotas, reduced tariffs and cut export taxes on agricultural products (Berry, 1997). While wages decreased, the government continued to spend substantially on both military and public projects that helped to offset the impact of increasing inequality in income.

South American countries now adhere to open trade agreements that have, over time, blunted many of the effects of the free-market reforms undertaken during periods of great economic stress. Trade and labor-unions have recovered some of their previous standing in a number of the countries, and governments have adopted a much greater concern for strengthening the social fabric of society. Recent emphasis on citizen participation in economic affairs has moved capacity-building activities to sub-regional and municipal levels where economic decision-making now has become as important at the local level as it is at the national and international policy-implementation level.

POLITICAL ALLIANCES

South America has experienced its share of sub-regional alliances since the Wars of Independence from Spain of 1810–1825. Political aspirations that translate into military, economic, or social alliances have arisen on numerous occasions, most notably involving Bolivia, Ecuador, and Venezuela in recent times. Cuba has also exerted an important influence in the area of health, where human performance has been greatly enhanced in many rural communities across South America.

A central element that has fueled nationalization as a political trend is most evident in the Andean communities of Bolivia and Ecuador. In these cases abundant natural gas in Bolivia and petroleum in Ecuador have raised issues of sovereignty over natural resources. Similarly, Venezuela has come to use its oil production as a force for societal change both at home and abroad. Recent bilateral talks and agreements between Caracas and Tehran and La Paz and Tehran have added a new ingredient to the South American political scene. This dialogue is viewed as a counterweight by some Leftist governments to the U.S.'s influence in South American economic and political affairs.

Bolivia

In September 2007, Iran's President Ahmadinejad offered to help Bolivia exploit its natural gas deposits with a $1 billion investment. The money would also support Bolivian initiatives in agriculture and construction, electricity generation, and the extraction of minerals (Clendenning, 2007). Bolivia has been a major supplier of tin since the 1870s (as well as silver and other minerals since the 1500s), and nationalized its tin mines after the popular revolution of 1952, prominently backed by the tin miners' militia (Weil et al., 1973).

Ecuador

Keeping with Ahmadinejad's desire to develop closer relations with Ecuador, Iran intended to establish its first embassy in Quito (Clendenning, 2007). Ecuador's President Correa is against a free-trade agreement with the United States, arguing that it is damaging to Ecuadorean industry, and has vowed to oppose a local USA military base. Correa threatens to cut ties with the IMF and the World Bank and to restructure the country's foreign debt. He claims that the country's oil wealth should be returned to the people. After his election in December 2006, Correa pledged to build low-cost homes and double the bonus that 1.2 million poor Ecuadoreans receive (BBC NEWS, 2006).

Venezuela

Venezuela "provides free or discounted oil to Central American and Caribbean countries. This country sends nearly 100,000 barrels a day to Cuba in exchange for "Doctors and Cuban Expertise on state security" (Rosenberg, 2007, p. 44). In addition, the country, through its ownership of CITGO, a U.S. refining and distribution company, gave $80 million worth of heating oil in winter to one of the poorest communities in New York City, the Bronx. While a third of Venezuela's oil is given away or subsidized, the remainder generally is sold in the United States. In the past, Venezuela's Chavez has pledged to help South American countries reduce their international debt by gifts of oil-generated funds, in addition to paying for millions worth of energy projects (Rosenberg, 2007).

Venezuela recently signed agreements with Iran to create a joint bank, a technical training program for the oil industry, and an industrial agreement. Previous agreements include building a jointly-owned petrochemical complex in Iran and another petrochemical complex in Venezuela that is already under construction (Karimi, 2007).

Cuban Health Initiatives

Another political alliance that has far-reaching ramifications for human performance in South America has been the emergence of Cuba's Latin American Medical School (ELAM) as a force for the betterment of health conditions among the poor across the continent. Established as a political strategy after Hurricane Mitch ravaged Honduras in 1998, Cuba sent teams of doctors and nurses to provide services to remote areas of Honduras where the population had little previous access to medical care (Field & Reed, 2006; Huish &Kirk, 2007).

Recognizing a potential for winning friends by expanding an earlier commitment to exporting medical services, Cuba developed a program of foreign aid that would train medical personnel in a six-year program. These participants would, in turn, return to their own communities or other underserved countries to provide medical services. Cuba would provide scholarships, living quarters, and small cash stipends to students, provided that the home country provided transportation. A micro-medical school program has also been developed where students are tutored by an established physician. This program requires students to participate in three days of classroom work and three days of supervised clinical work each week.

The first such medical class was established in 1999 in a former naval installation, and the university graduated 1,610 doctors in 2005. According to William Keck, Chair of the Department of Community Health Sciences at Northeastern Ohio Universities of medicine and former Executive Producer of ¡Salud! as well as a Peace Corps physician in Bolivia, as of August 2007 thirteen U.S. students had attended the Cuban university; one has passed some of her medical exams in the United States while another will have to retake her first medical boards (Field & Reed, 2006; personal communication, August 18, 2007).

The graduate practice relies on the Cuban community medical service model, where a single doctor and nurse are assigned to a specific neighborhood. They are responsible for examining every resident in the local community, developing patient histories and maintaining records for immunizations and other preventive care. The majority of the "international students are recruited from underserved communities—from poor, remote, marginalized and indigenous populations" (Medical Education Cooperation with Cuba (MEDICC), 2007, ¶9).

The curriculum also includes an emphasis in tropical and infectious diseases that are common to many Latin American countries. For example,

Melia (2007) reports that dengue fever has spread across Latin America "in one of the worst outbreaks in decades, causing agonizing joint pain for hundreds of thousands of people and killing nearly 200 so far this year" (p. 14A). According to the Pan American Health Organization, 630,356 dengue cases have been reported in the Americas, mainly in Brazil, Venezuela, and Colombia, with 12,147 cases of hemorrhagic fever (p. 14A).

The OECD Regional Partnerships

The Organisation for Economic Co-Operation and Development (OECD) adopted policy changes in 2001 to foster a greater regional approach to development in Latin America (Organisation for Economic Co-Operation and Development, 2007). Activities were proposed in the areas of "agriculture policy reform, anti-corruption and competition policy, corporate governance, education, environmental policies, labour market policies, international tax co-operation, investment policies, and statistical research" (¶1). OECD sponsorship has also maintained selected bilateral approaches, such as the Environmental Performance Review of Chile and the Review of Agricultural Policies in Brazil. The OECD also has invited signatories to its Anti-Bribery Convention (¶2).

NON-GOVERNMENTAL ORGANIZATIONS

Both international and domestic non-governmental organizations (NGOs) can help to bring about the system change that will either ameliorate barriers to human performance or empower individuals and communities in their search for more than a subsistence living. An international NGO can approach state ministries on an institutional level, while emerging citizen groups can move municipalities to respond to legitimate needs for local services. Neighborhood and village citizen coalitions as well as groups uniting in coalitions to further jointly-held interest have been gaining in popularity and influence. Citizen involvement, however, had been a common theme in development long before the president of the World Bank called for their renewed participation in projects.

WANGO

The World Association of Non-Governmental Organizations (WANGO), formed in 2000, is a coalition of international NGO member organizations, along with associate members of governmental and intergovernmental bodies, businesses, and universities. WANGO sponsors conferences, symposia, and forums where leaders from NGOs and other organizations share research and information about issues of global interest that transcend political, cultural, religious, race and ethnic boundaries (World Association of Non-Governmental Organizations, 2006). WANGO lists 892 member organizations in South America.

Union of International Associations

Another global collaborative is the Union of International Associations (UIA). UIA was formed in 1907 as a scientific research institute and documentation center. Its primary purpose is to encourage the evolution of international civil society through providing information to international organizations about developmental philosophies, objectives, and activities. UIA maintains online databases that provide access to information about world problems, global strategies, human development, and so on (Union of International Associations, 2007).

Heifer Project International

An example of an NGO working to increase human performance in South America, as well as on other continents, is Heifer Project International (HPI). Formed by missionaries in the 1940s, the organization is dedicated to building capacity through local projects focused on developing sustainable food and income production. Based on the concept of "passing the gift," HPI provides seed animals and education about care and maintenance, helping individuals develop skills in sheltering, healthcare, and reproductive management. Families who successfully manage their husbandry enterprise will in turn gift an animal to another family, retaining ownership over subsequent progeny. HPI practices "participatory decision-making," one of the "cornerstone" values foundational to the organization's philosophy (Heifer Project International, n.d.).

The organization also seeks to empower women where practical, providing them formal, contractual ownership of animals. Individuals and communities are guided by program staff available in the host country. Many communities adopt a cooperative model, often working with nearby communities to leverage marketing and other economic advantages. According to Dwight Steen, farmer, Peace Corps worker in Bolivia and USAID worker in Latin America, HPI has a history of collaborating with other developmental efforts, such as with local Peace Corps agricultural programs to further leverage community resources (personal communication, August 17, 2007).

Via Campesina

Via Campesina, founded in 1966, is a coalition of peasant and farm organizations made up of indigenous groups. According to Stromquist (2002), the organization:

> works for agrarian reform, with the objective of protecting women's contributions to food production, implementing agrarian reform to return territories to indigenous people, and granting landless and farming people ownership and control of the land they work as a means to avoid dislocation, forced urbanization, and repression of peasants. (p. 168)

The Inter-American Development Bank and Instituto Indigenista Interamericano report that there are 400 indigenous peoples in Latin America comprising a population of approximately forty million (Stromquist, 2002). In Andean Bolivia, Peru, and Ecuador, indigenous populations represent about half or more of the population.

GRASSROOTS DEVELOPMENT

An important measure of growth in human performance capacity is the increased ability of previously impoverished populations to rise above subsistence living, to better their conditions both nutritionally and economically. Grassroots development, whether aided by an NGO, the state, municipality, intergovernmental cooperation, or local coalition in their provision of an improvement vehicle, rely nonetheless on the initiative, persistence, creativity, and industry of individuals and communities to bring development concepts to fruition. The following examples illustrate how international, governmental, and local organizational efforts are building leadership, confronting poverty, and transforming communities across the South American continent.

Argentina/Bolivia

The Asociación de Mujeres Warmi Sayajsuqno (Warmi), founded in 1996, created a microcredit and enterprise development program with seed funds from an international NGO in 2001 in the Andean Puna plain of northwestern Argentina. Most Puna residents in Argentina barely subsist from agriculture, livestock and crafts, with an average monthly income of $138 for a family of eight. Headquartered in Abra Pampa, Warmi created 70 communal banks to serve tiny hamlets in the surrounding territory. According to Boyer (2006), besides having made 1,500 loans with a perfect repayment rate, Warmi "has invested in a gas station, a restaurant, a chinchilla farm, a textile and crafts store, a cyber café, and a depot for sheep wool and llama fiber that allows producers to bypass middlemen" (p. 35).

Abra Pampa is located at the convergence of roads from Argentina, Chile and Bolivia. Travel in this area ignores borders; "often, it is easier to go through Abra Pampa than to take a direct route between two points in Bolivia" (p. 35). Warmi has extended its influence to San Antonio de Esmoruco, an isolated village in the department of Potosí, Bolivia, whose weavers from San Antonio are now training in Warmi's workshops and learning the intricacies of developing a communal bank, themselves, to support their wool and textile manufacturing as well as marketing efforts in greater Bolivia.

Bolivia

Lanao Flore Aquiles and John Hatch created a consulting organization that channeled USAID funds to provide aid to rural communities. Their work led to the Foundation for International Community Assistance (FINCA—Spanish for farm), where they hoped to bring a local banking methodology to rural Latin America (Healy, 2006).

In contrast to a state agricultural bank or other bureaucracy, FINCA Bolivia allowed communities to create their own systems to document and officially approve loan records. "A community assembly delivered the loan, which encouraged transparency [and] FINCA required that ... 20 percent of each loan [be deposited] into a savings account to earn interest that would become an additional source of credit" (p. 42).

According to Healy (2006), the Bolivia program involved 300 communities from seven mountainous regions, straining the ability of FINCA to manage the organization. Also, borrowers could repay loans in kind, adding a complexity that required FINCA to market goods such as potatoes and sheep. "While repayment in kind helped index the value of the loan during Bolivia's hyperinflation, marketing," said Aquiles, "was incredibly complex and overwhelming, much more than anticipated" (p.42) (Refer to Peru, below, for more information about the highly- respected FINCA initiatives.)

Brazil

Santana, Brazil, in the state of Rio de Janeiro, is a community of African descendants whose residents, "like those of many other quilombos throughout Brazil, live in extreme poverty, marginalized from the local economy and society, and have scant access to health, education and other services" (Brandao, 2007, p. 17). They live from subsistence farming or by seasonal employment in nearby farms. Homes are typically made from adobe without floors. "Families cook on wood stoves; there is no treated or running water; [and] outhouses are the norm" (p. 19).

The government's literacy program, Brasil Alfabetizado, accommodated a group of 21 in 2004 from Santana to learn how to read and write. From their success, residents sought help to better their economic condition. The Federation of Industries of Rio de Janeiro (FIRJAN) responded, with collaborative funding from an international NGO, to train men from the community in carpentry, bricklaying, plumbing, and electrical installation and to raise their production of corn, beans, pumpkins, cassava and okra. The economic development also helped the local handicraft industry, where the community's women craft items from banana leaves. The FIRJAN program also addressed other community issues in its support for athletic and cultural activities for children and teens, and healthcare services (Brandao, 2007). Santana residents currently seek greater ownership of land to expand their limited farming capacity.

Colombia

In Barrio Las Marías, on the edge of Bogotá, the Asociación de Recicladores Las Marías represents some of the more than 100,000 Colombians who make a living recycling trash. According to Breslin (2002), "recycling by itself offers a future of continued and probably deepening poverty. People turn to it because they have little training and, consequently, few options" (p. 26). One estimate has it that recyclers earn about what they would selling newspapers or lottery tickets on the street. Compared with the available alternatives though, recycling offers more independence and an immediate payoff. The Asociación de Recicladores Las Marías is a member organization of the Asociación de Recicladores de Bogotá, a network of 22 similar groups, assisted by the Colombian NGO Fundación Corona. Corona helped the network find a headquarters that contains a day care center as well as provide loans and advice to neighborhood organizations (Breslin, 2002).

Corona helped train the Asociación's leaders in management, administration, research, and informational presentation techniques that they were able to use in city deliberations regarding city services related to garbage collection recycling. "The industry was modernizing; clearly, the recyclers had to adapt or be excluded" (Breslin, 2002, p. 28). The Asociación later won an exclusive 10-year contract to staff certain recycling centers in Bogotá. The organization has thus transformed recycling:

from itinerant scavenging into a business. Its centers provide steady jobs and salaries for many recyclers, but for recycling to be profitable, workers need to provide new services. . . . Leaders envision opportunities for Asociación members in reforesting urban green zones as well as in negotiating janitorial and other contracts with the city and private businesses. (p. 28)

Ecuador

In Esmeraldas, Ecuador, the Fundación Para La Tecnología y el Desarrollo Latinoamericano-Ecuatoriano (FTDE), an NGO based in the capital city, Quito has been helping more than 30 rural communities confront extreme poverty. FTDE brought together 540 residents to confront local problems. FTDE received a grant from the Inter-American Foundation to help residents develop alternative agricultural practices along with community development activities to strengthen local society (Schilken, 2007).

Esmeraldas communities are characterized by ethnic Afro-Ecuardorians, who, according to Schilken (2007) "are struggling to get their basic needs recognized and addressed by local, regional and national authorities" (p. 14). FTDE has concentrated on leadership development, identifying "primary community promoters" who represented their communities, then helping another 40 "secondary community promoters" to develop community organizing skills as well as "agricultural techniques, micro-enterprise management and marketing" (p. 14). The training sessions also provide opportunities for social interaction where trainees, who range in age from teenager to senior citizen, can escape some of the isolation of their small farms.

Paraguay

The Asociación Afro-Paraguaya Kamba Cua (AAPKC) grew out of a protest in 1999 where young people lobbied for title to a hundred hectares promised to their families dating back to the Wars of Liberation of 1810–1825. According to Durbin (2007a), residents had occupied the land for decades, planting corn, sugar cane, tobacco, watermelons, and other vegetables. They maintained that the governments of Morinigo and Stroessner discriminated against the Afro-Paraguayans, giving most of the land to the government or other parties. AAPKC spearheaded an occupation of the lands they claimed were rightfully their community's. In 2006, the government granted a deed to one and one-half hectares. AAPKC is now engaged in activities to promote racial equality, human rights and economic development for African descendants in Paraguay where there are fears "about racial profiling, the practice of requiring photos with job applications and race-based admission to places of entertainment" (p. 27).

The AAPKC headquarters are located in a building added onto Kamba Cua's primary school with funding assistance from Germany and help from an African-American U.S. Peace Corps volunteer. The school had been built earlier by the community with support from the municipality after lobbying by the AAPKC; one grade was added per year (Durbin, 2007a).

Another African-American Peace Corps volunteer worked with AAPKC to help build economic capacity in Emboscada, where work in a rock quarry has been the primary employment available to Emboscada men. According to Durbin (2007a), only a handful of Emboscada's African descendents have had any higher education. Described in a recent article in Asunción's ABC Digital, "many pedreros die before they are 40, from respiratory problems caused by inhaling thick dust as they smash the rocks into smaller pieces. The use of dynamite damages their hearing and causes serious, sometimes fatal accidents" (p. 29).

In a collaboration with the University of Asuncion, Paraguay's National Institute of Statistics and Organizaciones Mundo Afro of Uruguay, AAPKC looks to "help Afro-Paraguayans begin a dialogue with the government on public policies and programs and on an ethnicity component in the national census" (p. 29) through surveys administered in three Afro-Paraguayan communities.

Peru

The Andes have long been noted for rich weaving—scarves, sweaters, ponchos, mittens, and a host of other products have come primarily from sheep, llama and alpaca wool. The craft has declined in recent years, according to Breslin (2007), where mass production of clothing and other textiles as well as synthetic yarn and dyes, compromised the cottage industry. Further, worsening economic conditions spawned an exodus from rural areas, where the craft was handed down largely from mother to daughter. "Even the popularity of the weavings created a problem. Backpacking tourists bought up so many in some communities that there were few models left to inspire fledgling weavers" (p. 48).

The Center of Traditional Textiles of Cusco (CTTC) was founded in 1996 to generate more income for weaving communities. CTTC staff works with local weavers to help them recover traditional weaving techniques. The organization then markets the textiles as art, gaining higher prices both in Peru and abroad. CTTC maintains a museum and shop in Cusco, near the central plaza. Its training facility teaches leadership and management as well as weaving and has a sophisticated sales operation, including involvement in international trade fairs and exhibitions, as well as a bilingual web site (Breslin, 2007). The program serves about 350 weavers of both genders in nine Andean communities, where craftspeople create in their own traditional designs, then ship the product back to Cuzco for marketing. Proceeds from the weaving industry supplement subsistence farming and other household economic activities, thus enabling parents to have more resources to spend on education or basic necessities.

Another grassroots project is the FINCA, Peru offshoot of FINCA, International (*see* Bolivia, above) that merits attention for its work in Peru. The FINCA program in Peru has been working for more than 20 years to empower women by teaching sound fiscal practices through the community bank vehicle. Their concept, according to Healy (2006), is to gather women in groups of 20 to 30, where they borrow funds "over established lending cycles and also pool their savings to increase loan capital" (p. 40). Lanao Flore Aquiles, a member of the Peruvian Peace Corps staff, began promoting savings and loan cooperatives more than forty years ago based on a model developed by a Maryknoll missionary, and used prior experience in Bolivia to refine the concept. Aquiles was the principal drafter of Peru's first Cooperative Law.

FINCA's model uses two loan accounts, one external and the other internal, for each communal bank. FINCA's external account was funded by international donors (Healy, 2006). The internal account was funded by member savings, both voluntary and compulsory, and also from repayments transferred from FINCA's external account. The internal account was managed by communal bank members. As savings accumulated, the internal account became FINCA Peru's primary source of loans. Each female banker receives an initial loan of $50, repaid with interest in weekly installments, after which the loan amount may increase. "FINCA Peru centers its capacity-building around a weekly meeting held by each communal bank over a 16-week loan cycle, where members look at transactions and investment decisions and participate in hands-on training. "From the first meeting, FINCA Peru's promoters strive to instill the self-confidence essential to mastering the skills of village banking and to broader human development" (p. 44).

Some borrowers took advantage of contacts with farming communities to link rural producers with wholesale dealers and retail markets connected to urban consumers, becoming wholesalers in their own right. According to a report commissioned by the IAF (Healy, 2006), FINCA Peru's goal of generating new communal banks had been met, the researcher found that loans and savings tended to exceed initial targets and:

> also documented increased investments in gas stoves, refrigerators and sewing machines; all of the [female members] owned televisions, radios and mu-

sic players. Village banking accounted for improved housing, using cement and bricks, with plumbing services, potable water systems and electrical energy...59 percent of the women involved with FINCA Peru had stood up and spoken in public for the first time in their lives. (p. 46)

Another successful byproduct of the program is a new interest in savings. In Ayacucho, savings have generated between 13 percent and 15 percent in annual returns, and the internal account is three times greater that the external account. Aquiles claims that poor people can save, and "if we do not accomplish that in Peru, we will never escape widespread poverty,... waiting for the next round of gifts, donations and hand-outs. Savings must become a habit for genuine grassroots development to take place." (p. 47)

Uruguay

Organizaciones Mundo Afro also services Rivera, a town that straddles the border between Uruguay and Brazil. Mundo Afro sponsors Adán Parreño, an activist who developed a sports program to occupy the attention of youths 12 to 18 years old, most from single-parent households, and a number of whom live on the streets. The program features training, contests, local recognition and prizes donated by local government (Durbin, 2007b).

Mundo Afro Rivera also sponsors a vocational school where students learn to craft and play drums according to local custom. With a contingent of accompanying dancers, the goal of the organization is to become self-supporting by providing a tourist experience in Afro-Uruguayan heritage.

Nearby, Enilda Cruz Martins, a teacher, leads the Centro Cultural Zumbi dos Palmares. Cruz Martins creates African remedies from plants in her own garden, a business for which Mundo Afro has provided training in micro-enterprise strategies. Mundo Afro has also addressed issues of gender, health and education in the communities it serves. In addition to its efforts to keep children off the streets, the Centro Cultural has established another program to help "single mothers develop a source of income through classes in computer skills, recycling bottles and newspapers into crafts, and ceramics" (p. 34).

Venezuela

Under President Hugo Chavez, Venezuela's oil revenues have been converted into social programs through the "missions." According to Bernardo Alvarez, Venezuela ambassador to Washington, "We are doing what the old regimes didn't do...our first priority is a fight against poverty and exclusion; Today, oil money feeds and educates poor neighborhoods" (in Rosenberg, 2007, pp. 44–45).

While one mission teaches people to read, another sends Cuban doctors to poor neighborhoods around the country. Another mission subsidizes food and medicines, while the government issues identity cards to the undocumented. Mark Weisbrot from the Center for Economic and Policy Research sees the Venezuelan commitment as "an investment in human capital... [there is] a focus on food and health care and education. It doesn't cost that much, and it's reaching a lot of people" (as cited in Rosenberg, 2007, p. 78). Chavez's stated goal is to reach "zero misery."

The Venezuelan experiment in socialism is a work in progress, however. According to Rosenberg, while those living in extreme poverty has dropped from 20.3% in 1998 to 11.1% at the end of 2006, the percentage of those living without running water and in poor housing, and the number of children not attending school, has not budged for 10 years. At the same time, notwithstanding the infusion of trained medical personnel from Cuba, according to government statistics, "the percentage of babies born with low birth weights actually rose from 1999 to 2006" (p. 78).

EVALUATING GRASSROOTS DEVELOPMENT

An essential ingredient evident from the history and case studies presented here is the presence of collaboration, whether between NGO and community, government and community, or a coalition of local organizations. Research undertaken under the auspices of the Inter-American Foundation by the Education Development Center of Newton, Massachusetts (Levinger, 2002), has presented a model of partnership that speaks to the conditions that might be basic to sustainable development in a Latin American context.

As described by Levinger (2002), the research examined 12 successful partnerships in five countries in Latin America. The membership included NGOs, local municipalities, private businesses, government agencies and community-based organizations. The study sought to identify challenges faced by the partnerships "as well as the benefits they generated to learn more about the conditions that lead to productive partnering... [and] to gain insights into how such partnering might contribute to improving the lives of the marginalized and vulnerable" (p. 44).

Many NGOs now see partnering as a strategy that responds to community needs in developing countries by integrating community-based groups, corporations and local government into NGO projects. Such arrangements are thought to stimulate creativity and garner greater access to private resources (Levinger, 2002). The research found that partnership functions rather than outcomes contributed most to success. "Most successful partnerships do not have formal hierarchical structures, nor are they generally bound by legal contracts. Instead, these partnerships are built on strong trust that ensures accountability among participants" (p. 44). Written contracts were seen as indicative of a weak partnership and questionable commitment. Only where development funds were at stake, or where one partner was in charge of training another, was the formality of written contracts expected.

Partnership Conceptual Framework

The research suggested a framework of five variables that would define partnerships supportive to sustainability (Levinger, 2002):

- service delivery: activities at the grassroots level, with the full participation of the poor, to improve the quality of life—economic, social, or personal;
- human resource development: the empowerment that builds the skills of disadvantaged people or an organizational capacity;
- resource mobilization: securing financial and technical support needed to conduct project-related activities of service delivery, training, research, advocacy, evaluation and dissemination of successful practices;
- research and innovation: the testing and evaluation by participants and developers to assess the effectiveness of new strategies that respond to needs and problems;
- public information, education and advocacy: the dissemination and furthering of successful service delivery based on research and field-based experience. (p. 45)

Stages of Partnership

Finally, researchers defined five stages that characterized successful partnership relationships (Levinger, 2002), that "do not evolve through discrete, sequential phases; instead, they develop via a fluid, iterative process of back and forth movement across four stages" (p. 46):

- potential partnership: while aware of each other, they do not work closely together;
- nascent partnership: there is partnering, but efficiency is not yet maximized;

- complementary partnership:　partners derive benefits and increased impact through greater attention to a fixed and relatively limited set of domains; and,
- synergistic partnership:　partners derive benefits and increased impact, dealing with complex, systemic problems by adding new activities. (p. 47)

A partnership model can potentially help evaluators and program participants quickly identify and respond to project challenges with strategies to move grassroots development projects forward.

SUMMARY

Human performance improvement in South America has been subject to a wide range of variables. The tremendous growth of international trade and competition in the second half of the twentieth century forced non-industrialized countries to redefine their economic systems. The free-market policies of global capital, investment, and trade organizations imposed stringent requirements that for many South American countries resulted in fewer controls over business, lowered tariffs, less protection for workers, and increases in income disparity. The wealthy and their political allies benefitted, while urban laborers and rural farmers suffered. The global forces that can create successful economic activity can also create barriers to that success that worsen the status of the poor.

The paradoxes referred to in the chapter introduction demonstrate the mixed blessings that may attend political and economic revolution, where a transition to contemporary global standards of free-market trade has resulted in an increasingly unfettered movement of business activity, capital, and people across continents and borders. That process has created winners and losers, forcing governments to selectively reinstate economic controls and, finally, to join with communities where human performance development at the grassroots level has become the principal means to improve the conditions of the poor. While NGOs have for generations addressed local development issues, it is only recently that international and regional alliances have committed more substantial resources to local development.

International and domestic NGOs, regional trade groups, governments, and local cooperatives now see in collaboration the necessary and ideal vehicle for the betterment of impoverished communities in South America. They have come to recognize that the partnering of organizations, both great and small, can help people at the most basic level of society learn how to exploit their own resources and intellect, to develop leaders, and to provide for their families and communities through the capacity building represented in grassroots initiatives.

REFERENCES

Andean Community General Secretariat. (2006). *Ecuador's President calls for universal survival pact*. Retrieved November 20, 2007, from: http://www.comunidada-ndina.org/endex.htm

BBC NEWS. (2006, November 27). *Profile, Ecuador's Rafael Correa*. BBC NEWS:UK electronic version. Retrieved November 22, 2007, from http://news.bbc.co.uk/2/hi/americas/6187364.stm

Berry, A. (1997). The income distribution threat in Latin America. *Latin American Research Review, 32*(2), 3–40.

Boyer, G. (2006). Crossing a border in the Andes. *Grassroots Development, Journal of the Inter-American Foundation, 27*(1), 35.

Brandao, M. E. (2007). Land and autonomy in Quilombo Santana. *Grassroots Development, Journal of the Inter-American Foundation, 28*(1), 16–20.

Breslin, P. (2002). Bogota's recyclers find a niche—and respect. *Grassroots Development, Journal of Inter-American Foundation 23*(1), 26–32.

Breslin, P. (2007). Development and heritage in Cusco, Peru. *Grassroots Development, Journal of the Inter-American Foundation, 28*(1), 48–51.

Clendenning, A. (2007, September 28). Iranian President pays courting call in South America. *Arkansas Democrat Gazette*, p. A7.

Devlin, R., & Vodusek, Z. (2005, February). *Trade related capacity building: An overview in the context of Latin American trade policy and the MERCOSUR-EU association agreement*. Inter-American Development Bank, Integration and Regional Programs Department, Occasional Paper 29, Buenos Aires.

Durbin, P. (2007a). Afro-Paraguayans: Identity, synergy, census. *Grassroots Development, Journal of the Inter-American Foundation, 28*(1), 26–29.

Durbin, P. (2007b). Beyond Montevideo: Mundo Afro Rivera. *Grassroots Development, Journal of the Inter-American Foundation, 28*(1), 33–34.

European Union: External Relations. (n.d.). *The EU's relations with MERCOSUR*. Retrieved November 20, 2007, from: http://ec.europa.eu/external_relations/mercosur/intro/index.htm

Field, C., & Reed, G. (2006). *¡Salud!* [DVD]. United States: MEDICC.

Healy, K. (2006). Ayachucho's super savers: Village banking pioneers in the Peruvian Andes. *Grassroots Development, Journal of the Inter-American Foundation 27*(1), 40–47.

Heifer Project International (HPI). (n.d.). *Passing on the gift*. Retrieved November 24, 2007, from: http://www.heifer.org/site/c.edJRKQNiFiG/b.201546/

Huish, R., & Kirk, J. M. (2007). Cuban medical internationalism and the development of the Latin American school of medicine. *Latin American Perspectives, 34*(6), 77–92.

Hurtado, A. G. (2006). Development in Chile 1990–2005: Lessons from a positive experience. *Research Paper No. 2006/13, World Institute for Development Economics Research,* United Nations University, Helsinki.

Karimi, N. (2007, November 20). 2 allies in OPEC aim to see US slide with the dollar. *Arkansas Democrat Gazette*, p. A6.

Krueger, C. (2002). First steps toward poverty reduction in Bolivia. *Grassroots Development, Journal of the Inter-American Foundation, 23*(1), 40–41.

Levinger, B. (2002). Partnering for sustainable development in Latin America. *Grassroots Development, Journal of the Inter-American Foundation, 23*(1), 44–48.

Medical Education Cooperation with Cuba (MEDICC). (2007). *Latin American medical school.* Retrieved November 24, 2007, from: http://www.saludthefilm.net/ns/elam.html

Melia, M. (2007, September 30). Dengue epidemic surges in Latin America, Caribbean. *Arkansas Democrat Gazette*, p. A14.

Molyneux, M., (2002). Gender and the silences of social capital: Lessons from Latin America. *Development and Change 33*(2), 167–188.

Organisation for Economic Co-Operation and Development (OECD). (2007). *Partners: Inter-American development bank, organisation for economic co-operation and development.* Retrieved November 18, 2007, from: http://www.oecd.org/document/29/

Rosenberg, T. (2007, November 4). Can Hugo Chavez's 'oil socialism' show resource-rich countries the way to stability and prosperity? Or is it just the old oil curse in a new guise? *The New York Times Magazine*, 42–49, 78–80.

Schilken, M. (2007). More options in Esmeraldas. *Grassroots Development, Journal of the Inter-American Foundation, 28*(1), 14–15.

Stromquist, N. P. (2002). *Education in a globalized world: The connectivity of economic power, technology, and knowledge.* Boston: Rowman & Littlefield.

Union of International Associations. (2007). *About the UIA.* Retrieved November 24, 2007, from: http://www.uia.be/en/about

USAID Office of Population: Public Health Institute (n.d.).What is human performance technology (HPT)? Retrieved November 19, 2007, from: http/web/utk.edu/~cis/htp/hpt%20defined.pdf

Weil, T. E., Black, J. K., Blutstein, H. I., Hoyer, H. J., Johnston, K. T., & McMorris, D. S. (1973). *Area handbook for Bolivia* (2nd ed.). Washington, DC: The American University.

World Association of Non-Governmental Organizations (WANGO). (2006). *About WANGO.* Retrieved November 24, 2007, from: http://www.wango.org/about.aspx

CHAPTER 7

HUMAN PERFORMANCE IN INDIA

Ramesh Chander Sharma

OVERVIEW

The focus of this chapter is to understand how Indians emphasize human performance in the fields of Information Technology (IT) and Information Technology Enterprise Solutions (ITES). It highlights the strategies used by them to improve human performance in varied agencies, especially by large corporations such as computer companies. It further deliberates upon of the Indian national policy toward improving human performance particular emphasis on the IT industry. Case studies of institutions and corporate rendering training, one of the important tools toward achieving optimum human performance, is also traced from the past to the existing prevalence of opportunities for training in the country. Challenges for improving human performance in terms of culture, needs and expectations are also addressed.

INTRODUCTION

The Indian Subcontinent in Asia has a rich political status enriched by its geographical, cultural and language diversity. Even after Independence in

Human Performance Models Revealed in the Global Context, pages 129–151
Copyright © 2009 by Information Age Publishing

129

1947, the role of the British in developing infrastructure and education in India is widely acknowledged. Globalization and liberalization have opened avenues for economic growth and now; India has risen to the level of being the world's second fastest growing economy. Rendering expertise in the field of railways to other countries has become a routine for India. Natural resources and academic expertise have facilitated India to do research in nuclear science and after signing a nuclear deal with the USA, India was ushered into the elite nuclear society.

HIGHER EDUCATION IN INDIA

Since independence, higher education in India has witnessed a rapid growth with the number of universities having gone up from 20 to 378, colleges from 500 to 18,064 and teachers from 15,000 to nearly 48 million. Consequent to this growth, a rise in the enrollment from a mere 0.5 million in 1950 to more than 11 million in 2006, and the gross enrollment ratio (GER) in higher education from 1% to 10% has been experienced. Diversification, with a marked shift in courses from the conventional disciplines to interdisciplinary in emergent areas, was also common. The private aided and unaided sector joined hands with the public institutions to play an important role in this expansion. The issue of expansion, inclusiveness, quality, academic reforms are given great emphasis in the Eleventh Plan, which sets a target GER of 15% by 2012. This goal is proposed to be achieved through an increase in the intake capacity of existing institutions and by establishment of new institutions. As a move in this direction, the Prime Minister of India has already announced 30 more central universities. Many privately managed educational institutions have been raised to the Status of Deemed Universities. The need for another revolution in modern education has been felt and hence the reforms in education need to be the key point in its agenda.

Social Indicators

The social indicators pertaining to India indicate a stage of progress in the past few decades, particularly more after liberalization of economy. A decline in the proportion of population living below poverty line from 45% in early 1980s to 26% in 2000, and an increase in the literacy rate from 43% in 1980s to 65% in 2001 has been the encouraging fact. In the international front, the growth of foreign exchange reserves from a mere $5.8 billion in 1991, to $204.934 billion as of May 2007 is also observed. In the international market, India, the largest democracy in the world is considered a material and bright economy, which has begun to gain a foothold in the financial arena too. The bloom in the Indian economy has facilitated foreign companies to set up shops on Indian turf, and to compete with them locally. Noteworthy changes in the IT and ITES sector are the establishment of BPO (Business Processing Outsourcing) and KPO (Knowledge Processing Outsourcing) in India. The existence of Indian businessmen among the global business giants is evident by cases of the takeover of Arcelor and Corus by Indians. Besides this, due to soaring economy, Europeans and Americans are coming to India to study and work in the BPO and IT industry. The number of foreign nationals working in India is estimated to be more than 50,000. In fact, more than 12,000 are registered at the IT hub of India-Bangalore, which is also the state capital of Karnataka.

As documented in the Approach Paper to the Eleventh Five-Year Plan and Economic Survey (2006–07), there is reduction in the incidence of poverty, rise in the proportion of literates in the population, greater life expectancy at birth, lower rate of infant mortality and maternal mortality and so on. A review of this progress (Govt. of India, 2007) is provided in Table 7.1.

However, in comparison with peer countries in real terms reveals that still much more is yet to be achieved. For instance, in regards to health, 47% of the children are underweight as compared to 10% in China. India is ranked 124 (out of 173 nations) on the Human Development Index. India is an agriculture-based country. More than 700 million Indians live in rural areas, of which around 190 million live below poverty line. In addition, 84% of people in villages are illiterate, thereby opening avenues for exploitation, bonded laborers and economically non-independent groups. Challenges for national development are posed by this high magnitude of varied problems.

TABLE 7.1 Indicators of Progress in Social Sector

Indicators	Units	Past year	Level	Recent year	Level
Per capita GNP	Rs.1993–94 prices	1990–91	7.321	2003–04	11,799
Incidence of poverty	% of population	1993–94	36	2004–05	27.8
Male literacy rate (> 7 years)	%	1991	64.1	2001	75.3
Female literacy rate (> 7 years)	%	1991	39.3	2001	53.7
Sex ratio (female/male)	Females/1000 males	1991	927	2001	93.3
Infant mortality rate	Per 1000 live births	1990	80	2004	62

Source: (Government of India, 2007)

As India celebrates 60 years of Independence (1947–2007), one can look back 60 years ago and at the same time look ahead at what it could be 60 years from now. The former nuclear scientist turned President, Abdul Kalam aspires to "vision 2020 India." This vision has become the challenge for India, the world's largest democracy. The challenges and hurdles envisioned mainly encircle the need to work out twists in infrastructure, equitable development and managing growth. Kalam (2003), in his vision for a developed India, dreamed of transforming India into a developed nation by 2020, using technology as a tool. He asserted that through technological innovations and software, India is destined to be a developed country. In order for this to happen, he identified five areas based on India's core competence, natural resources and talented manpower for integrated action to double the growth rate of GDP and realize the Vision of Developed India. These areas are: agriculture and agro food processing; infrastructure; education and healthcare; and information and communication technology. The potential tools for improving human performance, namely education, training and ICT need to be organized. Through proper networking of different agencies dealing with the above mentioned areas in a planned way would address such sociocultural issues as building basic amenities in the rural homes, providing minimum healthcare facilities at an accessible place, and bridging digital divide among the have and the have-nots.

IMPACT OF POPULATION ON COUNTRY'S GROWTH

The population of India put pressure on various forefronts, which is manifested, in different forms. The working age population is unlikely to peak before 2016 and hence, India's population has been termed a "demographic dividend." The increase in the working age population provides a massive opportunity to soar in the numbers employed. On the other side, the population of India can make India a "demographic liability," which is a reminder to grow by 8 to 10% per year to provide jobs for the expanding working-age population. Movement of the people from rural and semi-urban areas to urban areas is an indicator of growth posing certain debatable issues. Mega slums and challenges to quality of life and social harmony, and environmental impacts are the effects of urbanization.

A balanced demography in India is made evident by the 54% of the population below 25 years of age. However, imbalances in gender and income spread are more prominent. Food, education, training and employment are the main agenda of the nation. Policy makers need to address the issues of upward mobility, urbanization and industrialization, which are commonly identified risk factors. Besides managing the young population, the country needs to face the challenges of managing an aging population with inadequate economic sources for maintenance. They also need to rectify the skewed demography mainly due to a distorted gender ratio, which in turn effects societal change. For example, an increase in the number of men over women has led to less established family structures, moved to institution living rather than existing home structure, weak marriages with frequent changes of partners and children of different parent descent, potential health hazards and a decreasing morale of the society at large.

Faces of India

India has been portrayed by outsiders from the particular angle of view about specific issues. The various faces of India that are projected based on various perspectives are growing India, young India, unequal India, urbanizing India, and mega-city India. The various faces of India (World Economic Forum, 2007) are discussed below.

Growing India

India is a country of 1.1 billion people growing at 9% per annum. India ranks second in the world in terms of population. It is expected to be the most populous country by the year 2040. The demographic transition in the country is a sign that India is growing in numbers. The population increase with the increase in the quality of human resources will be highly beneficial both for the nation and the world (World Economic Forum, 2007, p. 6).

Young India

The number of Indians below 35 years of age is more than 700 million and those below 25 years of age exceed 550 million. In other words, nearly half of India's 1.1 billion people are below 25 years of age. A prominent young population is a prime indicator for a high potential working population (World Economic Forum, 2007, p. 6).

Old India

Despite a youthful population in India, it is home to the second largest number of older people in the world (after China). Thus, India has to take care of this unemployable force, whose quality of life in terms of health, and ability to maintain basic economic and living standards are either minimal or nil (World Economic Forum, 2007, p. 6).

Unequal India

The diversity as evident by the urban-rural divide and a north-south imbalance in India is accelerated by a rising income gap. The income inequity provides a clear picture that a quarter of India's population lives below the poverty line. The divide is further enhanced with most of them living on small farm lands without access to prevalent/new technology in terms of communication, transportation and irrigation to develop these lands into a cultivatable land (World Economic Forum, 2007, p. 6).

Urbanizing India

Even though almost 70% of Indians still reside in rural areas, migration to larger cities in recent decades has led to a drastic increase in the country's urban population. The sudden increase in the floating population has led to the threat of housing, sanitation and health in the already crowded urban places (World Economic Forum, 2007, p. 6).

Mega City India

Even though India accounts only for 2.42% of the total world area, around 18% of the world's population has made India their home. Overcrowding in places has led to satellite towns and merging of the suburban areas with the main cities, thus resulting in the emergence of mega cities (World Economic Forum, 2007, p. 6).

Aspirational India

With the dynamic of more nuclear families and more employed members in families, the increased spending power of the middle class has come to the forefront of discussions in India. It is estimated that the emerging middle class will surge tenfold, exceeding 500 million by 2025 commanding 60% of the country's spending power. This implies that the middle class will drive the consumer market (World Economic Forum, 2007, p. 6).

GLOBE TROTTING INDIANS

The increase in the literacy rate from a meager 12.2% in the year 1947, when India got her independence, has risen high enough to match global standards. The increase in the literacy standards is mainly due to prestigious institutions like the Indian Institutes of Technology (IIT), Indian Institutes of Management (IIM) and All India Institute of Medical Sciences (AIIMS) churning out thousands of employable technical experts every year. Their expertise is acknowledged in their recruitment into the service of various institutions across the world for exorbitant pay packages. All over the world, Indians are known for their skills and technology savvy brains. Warner (2000) noted that about one-third of the engineers in Silicon Valley (California) are of Indian descent, while more than 7% of the valley's high-tech firms are led by Indian CEOs. While addressing an issue devoted to in-depth coverage of Indian immigrants, he found that without Indian entrepreneurs, Silicon Valley would not be what it is today. It placed the wealth generated by them at $250 billion, more that half of India's current GDP. Recently, Indians have progressed in their academic know-how to enjoy a dominant position in the information technology (IT) industry.

The vision of India in 2020 as proposed by Dr. Abdul Kalam, rests on the belief that human resources are the most important determinants of overall development (Gupta, 2002a). Agricultural productivity and industrial quality in IT and biotechnology sectors, stimulating growth of manufactured and service exports, improved status of health and nutrition, domestic stability and quality of governance can be ensured by rendering greater coverage and better quality education at all levels from basic literacy to hitech science and technology. The education system should aim to abolish illiteracy, achieve 100% enrollment at primary and secondary levels, and broaden access to higher education and vocational training through both traditional and non-traditional delivery systems.

The rate of economic growth and the type and number of jobs to be created in the future will be determined by the knowledge and skill of the workforce in India. In comparison to levels of formal vocational training ranging from 28% in Mexico to 96% in Korea, only 5% of India's labor force in the 20–24 age range has undergone formal vocational training. The nation's employable skills can be enhanced by cataloging of the entire range of vocational skills required to support development coupled with the expansion of the nation's system of vocational training institutes, widening the range of vocational skills taught, and actively involving the private sector in the delivery of industry relevant skills. Computerized vocational centers run by private self-employed businesses, which amount to a national network of 50,000 or more, have the potential to deliver low- cost, high-quality training to 10 million workers every year (Gupta, 2002, p. 6).

A parallel effort is required to upgrade the skills of Indian farmers, who represent 56% of the total workforce. The need for the expansion and supplementation of a national network consisting of thousands of farm schools offering practical demonstration and training on lands leased from local community farmers to the existing system of 300 Krishi Vigyan Kendras (Scientific Centers for Farmers) is also expected to bridge the gap between theory and practice (Rai, 2004).

Long Term National IT Policy

The National IT Policy of India has a long term vision and consists of Action Plan Part-I and Part-II (Government of India, 1999). *"All the 108 recommendations of the IT Action Plan Part-I emphasize the policy framework required for creating an ambience for the accelerated flow of investment into the IT sector, with specific orientation toward the software industry. The Information Technology Action Plan Part-II furnishes 84 policy instruments for the development, manufacture and export of IT hardware. The Task Force advocated that the software industry and the hardware industry are two sides of a gold coin representing India emerging as a global IT super power."*

IT Human Resource Development

The development of human resources in information technology has been the key point in the long term national policies. The major Recommendations in this policy pertaining to human development performance, namely Recommendation 43, 44, 45, 48 (Government of India, 1999) are discussed below.

Recommendation 43:   IT companies will be encouraged to play a significant role in IT education, for which the following steps will be taken:

- IT HRD, including IT education and training, informal as well as non-formal sector, will be treated as a Service industry.
- Banks and financial institutions (FIs) will be allowed to float special bonds, to be called Vidya Dhan (Education Bonds), to raise capital for investment in the IT education and training sector. The investment in Vidya Dhan will be treated at par with infrastructure bonds.
- Banks and FIs will make these funds available to IT HRD companies and institutions at low interest rates as applicable to priority lending sector.
- Entrepreneurs, including NRIs, will be offered special financial packages, including venture capital, to set up IT education facilities by banks and FIs.
- IT HRD companies will engage themselves in industry oriented as well as basic research in specific areas relevant to achieving the growth targets set for the IT industry.

Recommendation 44:   To foster and encourage HRD entrepreneurship, the following promotional measures will be taken:

- With a view to bring stability to the sector by minimizing the rate of attrition of trained manpower from companies due to shortage of skilled manpower in the industry and be able to plan a massive growth in domestic as well as global market, IT HRD companies will be allowed to offer special financial incentives to its employees such as Employee Stock Option (ESOP) and Sweat Equity as per recommendations 58 and 59 in the IT Action Plan (Part-II).

- Special IT HRD entrepreneurship training programs will be organized by the IT HRD sector in collaboration with IIMs and other leading management institutes for entrepreneurs and financial institutions.

Recommendation 45: The following academic policies will be put in place:

- IT HRD policy will be evolved and implemented such that academic training is affordable for even the poor and should cover all parts of the country including rural areas.
- Special programs will be instituted to support/encourage the higher end of IT education.
- Institutes of national importance such as IITs and IIITs will be encouraged to establish virtual institutes, particularly in the area of advanced post graduate and continuing education programs in IT. These programs will support IT education and Research at other institutions in the country.
- The reward package for IT professionals (particularly teachers) should be upgraded to avoid temptation to migrate to other countries.

Recommendation 48: To encourage the worldwide trend of employment of women in the IT sector, the following promotional measures will be taken:

- Telecommuting will be allowed for professionally qualified women in IT to facilitate their continued association with their work place in case they are not able to attend to the job onsite on a regular basis due to family constraints. The companies to set up infrastructure at their homes to be able to telecommute will offer such women special loans/financial grants.
- Virtual institutes will develop special HRD programs to help educated women enter the field of IT-enabled services.
- Banks and FIs will offer special financial packages on a proactive basis to support enterprising and professionally qualified women to set up home-based IT services in various areas of IT-led economic activities.

FOCUS ON GLOBAL ISSUES: OUTSOURCING

Through its mergers and acquisitions extravaganza in the increasingly fast-paced global business arena, corporate India is presently soaring high.

It needs managers who can visualize and create perspectives beyond current boundaries to stay ahead in the race. These managers also need to be global managers who have to think about issues on international platforms stretched across demographics, geographies and cultures to meet and take advantage of business needs. India has the world's largest English-speaking population spurring dramatic growth in the computer software industry. In addition, since more than 30.32 million Indians were using the Internet in 2007 as compared to 23.60 million in 2006 (Dewan, 2007), modern communication technologies have changed the way business is transacted.

Because India has a critical mass of educated and skilled young men and women, some of the world's best institutions for study of science and technology, and the productive energies of a vibrant private sector, it has the necessary ingredients to become a technology-enabled country. Improving utilization, reducing sales and general expenses, and moving more businesses offshore are changes to be managed by Indian IT companies in order to continue to compete in the global environment. Integration of the Indian economy into the global economy on a much larger scale, in terms of import and export trade, capital flow on account of foreign direct investment or portfolio investment and integration of service sector, and inflow of remittance have been noted in the last decade.

Besides the economic changes, a variety of structural changes have been prominent with some of the Indian cities like New Delhi, Bangalore, Mumbai, Chennai and Hyderabad are fast emerging as destination for outsourcing of IT and business processes. The main reasons for this development of the global corporate world in India are process maturity which results in operational efficiency, availability of relevant skills at a cheaper price, and cost effectiveness for outsources, because of low establishment costs (NASSCOM-McKinsey Report, 2005).

Globalization coupled with the success of Indian software companies like Infosys, NIIT, Wipro, Satyam and others have made foreigners take notice of them, and join with them to learn the finer points of programming. Tata Consultancy Services (TCS) established back office in Guadalajara, Mexico in May 2007. TCS already has 5000 workers in Brazil, Chile and Uruguay. Cognizant Technology Solutions opened its back offices in Phoenix and Shanghai. Wipro has its offices in Canada, China, Portugal, Romania and Saudia Arabia, among other locations. Infosys is also establishing its back offices in Mexico, the Czech Republic, Thailand and China as well as low-cost regions of the United States. The Indian companies are outsourcing without Indians. In addition, India has become the learning ground for technical know-how. For example in Infosys there are American graduates who accepted a novel assignment of learning in India and then flying back home to work in the company's American back offices. Unisys

Global Services India (UGSI) offers a M-Tech internship program wherein the students and academia collaborate (Agarwal, 2006).

THE THREE PILLARS OF HUMAN PERFORMANCE

The three key pillars (Sharma, 2004) that support India's IT-BPO sectors are the following:

- the educational institutions
- the industry and
- the students.

In the existing environment, the country's educational institutions were a major resource for newly qualified graduates and postgraduates with a strong emphasis on mathematics and science. Consistent increase in the output of trained human power with a mastery over quantitative concepts coupled with English proficiency both at the degree/diploma level had been noted.

Due to the existence of high English skills among Indian students, their ability to be mobile, and their potential to learn, training at the worksite was possible. The Indian IT-ITES industries had high work ethics, were adaptable and customer responsive, had an inclination to learn and grow and were providing high quality, cost-effective services through a vast pool of skilled software workers drawn mainly from the local population (Hindu Business Line, 2007).

STRATEGIES FOR HUMAN PERFORMANCE

Indian companies are witnessing large growth, but continued aggressive growth requires good people to keep pushing beyond the edges. And to keep good people improving, ongoing professional training is a must. According to a study by the International Labor Organisation major companies are currently spending around 3% of their total payroll cost on training annually (International Labor Organisation, 2008). For example, Tata Consultancy Services (TCS) spends nearly 2% of its revenue on training (Mehta, 2008). In addition to the continuous training program on varied technologies, processes and domains, TCS also has leadership development programs. These programs are aimed at grooming and creating global managers who can serve as leaders and mentors for their teams (Tata Consultancy Services Ltd. (TCS), 2008). The in-house training programs have been preferred by Infosys Technologies (Shankar, 2005) and Accenture (Shergill, 2005). The Accenture's training curriculum consists of three parts: application delivery training, technical specialty training and professional development training. Individual career development is given great significance at the company.

Chunduri (2006) reported on the Neilsoft's Headstart program for the students of Tier 2 engineering schools as a part of the NASSCOM IT Workforce Development Initiative. Ravichandar (2006) reported that since 2003, large Indian IT companies have increased their employee strength by nearly 23%. He also revealed that of the global outsourced IT-BPO market, nearly 44% is represented by India. GCI (Global Consultants, Inc.) provides end-to-end information technology solutions to Fortune 500 and global mid-market enterprises, recognizes the performance of employees through various awards, like group awards, individual awards, long service awards, spot awards, cultural team events and awards, and sports club team and awards (Ravichandar, 2006). To promote bright individuals, the company has a mentorship/accelerated growth program under the supervision of senior managers (Gupta, 2006b).

Gupta (2006a) advocated the collaboration between academia and industry to improve the quality of professionals. He suggested that every company could adopt at least one engineering college to provide its students with industry knowledge. Joint examinations may be conducted to determine various levels of expertise, instead of merely providing fundamental knowledge about the discipline. A holistic approach should be adopted. For example, while teaching the students about programming languages, they need to be trained to write the scope, design, code, and unit test cases for a given problem. There is further need of having behavioral training in the curriculum as mandatory. In addition, soft skills, real life case studies, and international culture should be part of a core curriculum.

CASE STUDIES ON INSTITUTIONS BASED IN INDIA

Various Institutions in India have focused on rendering training for IT and ITES. Some are pure educational institutions and others are training centers located in the corporate setting. The Indian IT-ITES organizations could contribute to these strong centers in the following ways:

- Help in the design of relevant courseware.
- Help in the delivery of a course.
- Provide training in technical and soft skills while on campus.
- Encourage more institutionalized summer/winter internships.
- Provide Certification courses for faculty and students.
- Involve faculty in actual projects or provide consulting with faculty.

The Indian IT-ITES organizations that contribute to the training of Human resources suitable for the IT-ITES sectors can be classified into Educational Institutions and IT-ITES Companies which has a training wing.

The National Institute of Information Technology (NIIT)

The National Institute of Information Technology (NIIT) founded in 1981 in India is an international IT education and training institute and is one of the examples of India's software workforce training model. NIIT combines education, research and development into one organization, which was certified by BVQI of Britain ISO9001 in 1993. NIIT exists among the 1% of the companies in the world that can meet all the requirements of quality and timing in software development as certified by SEI-CMM5. At NIIT, which is all based on computer systems and internet, a strong team of IT professionals and experts lead the education and training.

Quality and practicality of IT training is ensured at NIIT by coupling its formal education with strong cooperation among IT companies, such as Microsoft, Sun, Oracle and Computer Associates (CA). This arrangement enables access to the most up-to-date information and technology from the real IT world. Training programs aim to provide advanced software knowledge, and inculcate abilities to work in any international software development environment.

The models prevalent in the training programs provided by NIIT are described below.

- The "case model," or "order model," of software personnel training is a combination of class education and business cooperation which exists in NIIT. This model can be analogized as a software product order where the class theory and practice are integrated so that knowledge and ability are qualified by real world practice.
- The NIIT-created MCLA (Model Centered Learning Architecture) model, which illustrates the whole process of software technology study, is based on case study and real problem solving approaches. MCLA is the keystone of the NIIT software-training model.
- Training in programming and technical development coupled with versatile abilities required by the fast changing IT industry is also prevalent in NIIT. This is made possible by way of a course called "ISAS" (Information Search and Analysis Skills).
- Faculty training targeting education theories, teaching methods or the specific technology course, content, and student feedback is provided to keep the teaching/learning process tuned to the prime requirement (NIIT, 2006).

NASSCOM Assessment of Competence (NAC):

National Association of Software and Service Companies (NASSCOM) is the premier trade body and the chamber of commerce for the IT software and services industries in India. NASSCOM Assessment of Competence (NAC) is a special initiative designed to sustain India's edge in the global BPO industry by creating a strong base of relevant human resources. During the pilot stage itself, NAC received an overwhelming response, with more than 6,000 people, 22 companies, state government and reputed educational institutions participating in the program. More than one lakh (100,000 in metric numerals) young job aspirants appeared for NAC in the first year of its national roll-out. The goal of the assessment and certification program, which is similar to the SAT, GMAT and GRE examinations, is also to meet the labor demand-supply gap the ITES-BPO industry is expected to face over the next decade. The initiative is also expected to help ITES-BPO players reduce their hiring costs, improve efficiencies, enlarge the candidate pool and reduce fluctuations in the entry-level wages. In the future, it will help align educational curriculum offered by universities and colleges in the country with the needs of the ITES-BPO sector.

NASSCOM recently announced a "Finishing Schools for Engineering Students" program, which is expected to enable young technical graduates to become industry-ready. On a pilot basis, eight institutions, including IIT Roorkee and seven NITs—Calicut, Durgapur, Kurukshetra, Jaipur, Surathkal, Trichy and Warangal are conducting the program. This pilot effort has twin objectives (NASSCOM, 2007):

- To empower young engineering graduates to gain job proficiencies through appropriate training.
- To make available a larger pool of suitable candidates for the IT industry.

The "Finishing Schools" cover the curriculum for technical (reinforcing some basic engineering skills and acquiring industry-specific knowledge) and soft skills development (for management and employment skills).

NASSCOM and the University Grants Commission (UGC) of India have collaborated to develop curricula relevant and oriented to industry with an aim to strengthen professional education through curricula, faculty, infrastructure, and pedagogy improvements.

Bannari Amman Institute of Technology (BIT)

BIT is an educational Institution located in Tamil Nadu. BIT has done significant work in terms of building an interface with the IT industry and gearing up its faculty to create relevant, and rightly skilled professionals. One of the key initiatives unveiled by BIT centers around Information

Technology-Faculty Training Programs (IT-FTP) on the technical subject matter of Java and Net. BIT has conducted these initiatives in association with NASSCOM and major IT industry leaders, Sun Microsystems and Microsoft (Bannari Amman Institute of Technology, 2008).

The Maveric Initiative

In order to take on the manpower and specialized skills challenge being faced by the testing industry, Maveric conceived and implemented unique industry-academia collaboration in early 2004 with the Management Development Centre of LIBA (Loyola Institute of Business Administration, a leading business school in the country). Through this partnership, Maveric Systems created a two-year Post Graduate Diploma in Software Testing. The program has been designed to create a breed of specialized professionals who have been groomed for a career in software testing.

Cincom Systems India

Cincom's state-of-the-art peer-to-peer communications platform also provides an organic system for fostering communications and knowledge sharing among branch offices around the world. All information is shared with everyone in the company, regardless of seniority, level, function, or "aura." In its open approach to address employees' queries, the company dedicates an Open House section known as "Heard a Humour" on its website for its employees to post any questions, to which they are entitled to receive a reply within seven days. This section provides latitude to all employees to voice opinions, be heard and feel valued.

The company prioritizes learning among its employees. In India, it has facilitated a tuition reimbursement policy for employees who wish to pursue skill enhancement programs. The reimbursement is of 0.2 million Indian Rupees (INR), open to all Cincom employees in India (Cincom, 2008).

Sapient

Sapient, a US-based, innovation-led ICT major provides solutions to global customers in the areas of business and IT planning, business applications, outsourcing, marketing services and business intelligence. Sapient has a robust in-house training strategy which is focused on closing the gaps in needed competencies, building cross-domain experiences and core value and skills that can be used by its people across the globe, creating external experiences with professional communities, developing existing and future leadership and delivering on responsibilities.

Liquid Krystal

The Liquid Krystal Company (2008) provides IT education to the masses through online learning solution. Its online academic learning exchange "gyanX" (based on CodeSaw technology) enables the students to advance their proficiency in industry-relevant skill sets. Liquid Krystal has entered into an agreement with the Visveswaraiah Technological University in Karnataka, India to train IT professionals in soft skills, programming skills and career skills.

Sasken Communication Technologies Limited

Sasken (established in 1989 as Silicon Automation Company) deals in telecom research and development outsourcing. It provides services to companies such as Nortel, Nokia and Motorola. They have offices in India, Canada, China, Germany, Japan, Sweden, UK, and the United States. Sasken (2008) works toward promoting five core values: Integrity, Respect for Individual, Innovation, customer Orientation and Excellence (IRISE) among its staff through educational and technical skill development programs.

Aspire Systems (India) Private Limited

Aspire Systems (2008), a leading outsourced product development company, provides services in the areas of new product development, product advancement, product re-engineering, product migration, product maintenance, product implementation, product testing, product support and product documentation. Continual learning opportunities in the form of inbound and outbound training programs for staff both on-the-job and off-the-job are provided in the technical and soft skills segments. The staff is also encouraged to participate in seminars and conferences. Aspire sponsors half of the costs toward any such training which staff members pursue to upgrade their technical skills.

Cognizant

Cognizant (2008) deals with offering RFID (Radio-frequency identification) solutions. To enhance human performance, the company provides in-house training and also has a resource pool of experts having prior working knowledge in RFID area.

Xansa (India) Limited

Xansa founded in 1962, is an international business process and IT services company creating and delivering process and technology solutions that significantly improve the business performance of customers. Xansa (India) Limited (founded in 1989) offers end-to-end services such as business and technology consulting, IT implementation, IT outsourcing and business process outsourcing across varied industries like banking, insurance, utilities, telecommunications and media, government, retail and consumer goods, aerospace and defense. Xansa (2008) conducts in-house training program in the form of an Induction program for new recruiters, local induction processes for those who are transferred from one project area to another. In addition special training programs are also conducted keeping in view the business exigencies.

Satyam Computer Services

Satyam Computer Services (2008) is an Indian origin IT company, and is the first Asian Company to be ranked among the top 25 global training organizations. An iterative approach to training is followed, whereby basic skills are taught to beginners and training provided to develop them consistently during their stay in the company. Training packages use a blend of e-learning and instructor-led coursework.

Tata Consultancy Services (TCS)

The company provides training based on the educational levels of the individuals so as to balance the roles and the available skill sets. Non-graduates are trained in basic IT and deployed for a spectrum of jobs in the basic level of ITES. In comparison, the Graduates in Arts and Science are trained for programming profiles and a part of the engineering and management teams are placed in software engineering activities.

Both "just-in-time training" (which is more reactive in nature and caters to the skills related to platform, technology, application domain, etc. specific to a project) and continuing education program (consistent with TCS' strategic thrust areas) is provided to the employees to reinforce the concepts learned during the education/induction training through on-the-job experience (Tata Consultancy Services Ltd. (TCS), 2008).

RURAL RETAILING TOWARD HUMAN PERFORMANCE

In India, more than 60% of the country's 1.1 billion population live in rural areas. The rural markets are growing at double the rate of urban markets. However, 87% of rural markets do not have access to any sort of organized marketing and distribution. Hence, currently, the retailing sector has been one of the fastest growing sectors in India. Customized credits in association with banks are the main thrust for retailing. The products on the rural retail shelf are generally agro-based. However, in reality, the companies are using strategies to make available products varying from cricket bats to customized credits in association with banks. In 2002, DCM Sriram launched its Hariyali Kisan Bazaar, and now, it has more than 70 stores. Adopting a low-cost and de-risk model, Indian Oil Corporation (IOC) launched its rural retail initiative in Uttar Pradesh, Madhya Pradesh, Punjab, Tamil Nadu, Karnataka and Bihar in 2006. It leverages on IOC network for fuel and non-fuel retail, with main thrust on agricultural inputs and Fast Moving Consumer Goods (FMCG) products. Tata Chemicals (TCL) launched its Tata Kisan Sansar (TKS) initiative in 2005 in fertilizer business. The corporations are taking special efforts to make sure the quality of products and services offered to rural customers are distributed over a wide area. The main challenges, which need to be taken seriously while dealing with rural retail, are issues such as poor infrastructure, seasonality of demand, heterogeneous population, complex buying behavior and price sensitivity.

CHALLENGES ENCOUNTERED

Cultural Differences

Each nation has its own soft skills and body language, which are accepted by its society. However, cross-cultural employment necessitates the awareness of practices most prevalent in the society where the individual is employed. For example, shaking hands is not encouraged in India whereas the individual working in the USA should get accustomed to the gesture of shaking hands—which implies acceptance and solidarity in American culture. This situation stresses the importance of cross cultural training. An example of including such cross cultural training is Wipro, the major Bangalore-based IT company (2008). This program includes cross cultural training, not just for its employees but also for its overseas clients. Through cross cultural training, mutual benefits are experienced by both these groups, as the ultimate role of employee is to rise to the expectation of the society's social practices.

Need Expectations

In spite of the abundance of available English-speaking talent in India, the required pronunciations and phrases of word usage are very different from that of native users. This calls for special training for Indians who already speak English. Similarly, all English speaking individuals cannot be employed in the IT sector, as the field needs specific skills as described below:

- Software analysts domain specialists, information security, integration specialists, database administrators, network specialists and communication engineers, data warehousing and semiconductor design specialists.
- People skilled in mainstream business applications such as systems packaging, virtualization, automated management, VoIP converged

devices, federated data, composite applications, Web services and on-the-horizon technologies such as Radio Frequency Identification (RFID), mesh networks and the semantic Web.

- Professionals (particularly in the BPO sector) skilled in higher-level technical support, account management, customer data analytics, among others.

Time Adjustment

Even though Greenwich Mean Time defines the time existing in the various countries in terms of the Indian Standard Time, most individuals working in IT/ITES are required to use the National time standard which has made strides in this field. For example, India follows UK and U.S. timings, which require individuals to work at night and rest during the day, which in turn affects work and family schedules and lifestyles. On the other hand, it also opens up work for people in certain situations such Indian Students, who study in a conventional educational institution during the part of the day. The money earned by coupling work and study have opened new vistas in financing continuing education and thereby better job prospects on the long run which in turn improves the economic stand of the individual.

The strategies for improving quality of life for all segments of the population would have to keep these challenges in view. The various elements of these strategies would be:

- design institutions that can help improve effectiveness of the programs,
- establish regulatory framework so that participation in service provision can be extended to private sector as well,
- exploit technology, and
- mobilize resources for meeting the goals.

FUTURE TRENDS

An average growth rate of 8.6% measured by the gross domestic product (GDP) has been experienced during the past few years in India. The report India@Risk 2007 was done jointly by the World Economic Forum's Global Risk Network and the Confederation of Indian Industry (CII) in the year 2007 (World Economic Forum, 2007). This report refers India as "a country characterized by huge opportunities and ever-increasing regional and global interdependence." This report gives the future trends of India. This report foresees the prospect of achieving a sustained growth rate of

8 to 10%. It also highlights numerous basic challenges that slow down development. Globalization coupled with better economy has led to better purchasing power of the middle class in India. This has stretched the existing infrastructure in India to its upper limits and calls for increased investment in infrastructure like better roads, housing, shopping complex, office accommodation and airports to better the society. Effective training programs to develop human resources in the areas of manufacturing skills and construction skills are on focus by the industries sandwiched with pay packages good enough to attract or retain the best talent.

The Eleventh plan of India (2007–2012) lays great emphasis on acceleration of economic growth. The impact of growing economic of human resource has led to the emergence of two distinct sectors, namely the social sector (health, education, housing and social welfare) and the economic sector (agriculture, industries and physical, infrastructure, etc.). Remarkable growth at the international level was prominent in India over the past two decades. The foreign exchange reserves have risen from $5.8 billion (in 1991) to $204.934 billion as of May 25, 2007. India has gained prominence in the international market. The ability to sustain the hold in the financial arena is the expected future trend of India. Constant updating of skills, reorienting education and training programs are essential to stir up the economic sectors in response to changing marked conditions.

The industry boom in India has facilitated India to become the destination for Europeans and Americans to study and work in the BPO and IT industry in Bangalore and Gurgaon. It is estimated that the number of foreign nationals working in India to be more than 50,000 with more than 12,000 registered at the IT hub of Bangalore. India and the companies based in India have taken the right step to train the existing workforce and thereby open avenues for India being not only a training center for IT and ITES but also the best bargain place for horizontal and vertical mobility. Leadership development, internal transfers, global opportunities, mentoring, two-way communication, training and reward systems coupled with world-class HR processes and policies which include a clear understanding of employee aspirations have been the common thread among the companies, which can be rated as the best employers in India.

The six risks confronting India, as highlighted by *India@Risk 2007* report (World Economic Forum, 2007), are the following: (1) Economic impact of demographic changes, (2) loss of freshwater; (3) economic shocks and oil peaks; (4) globalization versus protectionism; (5) climate change and challenges to India's growth; and (6) infectious diseases.

Collaboration targeted at collective action among the government, the private sector and the civil society on governance reforms to eliminate corruption and ensure equity in the provision of basic services (such as education, water and sanitation) is the need of the hour. It is noteworthy to mention that one of India's premier company's Larsen and Toubro (L&T) has opened a school dropout training center through its L&T Employees Trust to train people who could not complete their schooling. The purpose of this center is to impart skills that would make them useful in their villages, for example, be able to repair tractors, irrigational accessories, and motor pumps.

CONCLUSION

One of the key causes for the extraordinary growth of India's software industry is that India has developed an effective method of training an advanced and functional software workforce and turned it into a globally recognized model of such training. The Human performance in the IT and ITES sector in India is ensured both at the entry, on the job levels by the educational institutions and the IT companies. One of the strategies in this direction would be to design such curriculum in each of these categories which would open new horizons for India to be the training ground for personnel of the IT and ITES sector outside and inside India. Keeping this objective in view, the industries are focusing on effective training program to develop human resource in the area of manufacturing skills and construction skills. One of India's premier companies Larsen and Toubro, for example, have opened a school dropout training center through its L&T Employees Trust to train people who could not complete their schooling. Such people possess imparted skills that would make them useful in their villages, for example, be able to repair tractors.

REFERENCES

Agarwal, M. (2006). Eliminating the gap! *IT Industry Communiqué for the Academia, 1*(6), 4–5.

Aspire Systems. (2008). *Home page.* Retrieved June 2, 2008, from: http://www.aspire-sys.com.

Bannari Amman Institute of Technology (BAIT). (2008). *Home page.* Retrieved June 2, 2008, from: http://www.bitsathy.ac.in/

Cognizant. (2008). *Home page.* Retrieved June 2, 2008, from: http://www.cognizant.com/html/news/pressreleases/2006/indiainfra.asp.

Chunduri, P. (2006). Neilsoft's headstart program. *IT Industry Communiqué for the Academia, 1*(6), 5.

Cincom. (2008). *Home page.* Retrieved June 2, 2008, from: http://www.cincom.com/us/eng/index.jsp?loc=ind.

Dewan, N. (2007). *The most user friendly websites in India, June 5, 2007.* Retrieved June 2, 2008, from: http://www.juxtconsult.com/press_room/press_release/india_online_2007.asp

Government of India (1999). *Information Technology action plan.* Retrieved June 2, 2008, from http://it-taskforce.nic.in/actplan3/index.html

Government of India. (2007a). *Approach paper to the Eleventh Five-Year Plan.* New Delhi: Ministry of Finance, Government of India, New Delhi.

Government of India. (2007b). *Economic Survey 2006–2007.* New Delhi: Ministry of Finance, Government of India, New Delhi. Retrieved on June 2, 2008 from http://indiabudget.nic.in/es2006-07/tables.htm

Gupta, A. (2006a). Opportunities and challenges for academia and how industry can contribute! *IT Industry Communiqué for the Academia, 1* (5), 1–3.

Gupta, K. (2006b). Global consultants. *IT Industry Communiqué for the Academia, 1*(6), 5–7.

Gupta, S. P. (2002). *Report of the committee on India Vision 2020.* Planning Commission, New Delhi: Government of India, pp.6

Hindu Business Line. (2007, May 14). BPO Sector—Busting the myths, The Hindu Business Line. Retrieved on June 2, 2008 from: http://www.nasscom.in/Nasscom/templates/NormalPage.aspx?id=51495

International Labour Organization (ILO) (2008). *Learning and training for work in the knowledge society.* Retrieved June 2, 2008, from http://www.ilo.org/public/english/employment/skills/hrds/report/rep_toc.htm

Kalam, A. P. J. (2003). *Vision for a developed India.* Retrieved January 18, 2008, from: http://www.rediff.com/money/2003/nov/14spec.htm

Liquid Krystal Company. (2008). *Home page.* Retrieved June 2, 2008, from: http://www.liqwidkrystal.com/?mode=gyanx

Mehta, A. C. (2008). *Tata Consultancy Services Ltd.* (TCS). Retrieved 2 June 2008, from: http://www.moneycontrol.com/news_html_files/news_attachment/2008/Tata%20Consultancy%20Services%20Ltd.pdf

NASSCOM. (2007, May 5). *Education initiatives.* Retrieved June 2, 2008, from: http://www.nasscom.in/upload/5216/July%205%202007%20%20Education%20Initiatives-Final.doc

NASSCOM-McKinsey Report. (2005). *Extending India's leadership of the global IT and BPO industries.* Retrieved June 2, 2008, from: http://www.mckinsey.com/locations/india/mckinseyonindia/pdf/NASSCOM_McKinsey_Report_2005.pdf

National Institute of Information Technology. (2006). *Career programs.* Retrieved June 2, 2008, from: http://www.niit.com/ILB/India/asp/ILB_index.asp?Section=ILB&L1=Programs&L2=Career%20Programs&L3=Advantage

Rai. M. (2004, January - March). *ICAR News, 10*(1), 16. Retrieved June 2, 2008 from: http://www.icar.org.in/dipa/events/ICAR-NEWS/Volume_10/no_1/10-1.pdf

Ravichandar, H. (2006). Shaping India's talent pool. *IT Industry Communiqué for the Academia, 1*(6), 1–3.

Saken Communication Technologies Ltd. (2008). *Home page.* Retrieved June 2, 2008, from: http://www.sasken.com/

Sapiant. (2008). *Home page.* Retrieved June 2, 2008, from: http://www.sapient.com

Satyam Computer Services. (2008). *Home page*. Retrieved June 2, 2008, from: http://www.satyam.com

Shankar, R. (2005). Infosys technologies. *IT Industry Communiqué for the Academic Fraternity, 1*(3), 2–4.

Sharma, S. (2004, August). *BPO industry in India- A report*. Retrieved June 2, 2008 from: http://www.bpoindia.org/research/bpo-in-india.shtml

Shergill, P. (2005). Accenture India delivery center. *IT Industry Communiqué for the Academic Fraternity, 1*(3), 4–6.

Tata Consultancy Services Ltd. (TCS). (2008). *Home page*. Retrieved June 1, 2008, from: http://www.tcs.com/homepage/Pages/default.aspx

Warner, M. (2000, May 15). The Indians of Silicon Valley, *Fortune*, May 15, 2000. Retrieved January 18, 2008, from: http://money.cnn.com/magazines/fortune/fortune_archive/2000/05/15/279748/index.htm

WIPRO. (2008). *Home page*. Retrieved June 1, 2008, from: http://careers.wipro.com/workingwipro_mrajim.asp

World Economic Forum (2007). *India@Risk 2007*. India Economic Summit: A Global Risk Network and Confederation of Indian Industry Briefing. Geneva, pp. 6–7.

Xansa (India) Ltd. (2008). *Home page*. Retrieved June 1, 2008, from: http://www.xansa.com/industries/

ABOUT THE EDITORS

Kathleen P. King, EdD, is Professor of adult education at Fordham University Graduate School of Education in New York City. King major areas of research include transformative learning, professional development, distance learning, and instructional technology. Her experience in adult learning has spanned these fields in diverse organizations including community based organizations, business, higher education, career and technical education and numerous partnerships. Most recent endeavors continue to explore and develop learning innovations and opportunities to address equity, access and international issues. She has led the development of numerous local and global innovative adult learning projects some reaching over 3.6 million learners through technology; most of these efforts have been underwritten by corporate, federal and state grants.

Dr. King is the author of eleven books and over 100 published articles and research papers. Her books and web-based audio materials are used as course materials in universities around the world and have a large following. King is the editor in chief of *Perspectives, The New York Journal of Adult Learning,* research board member for several national and international academic journals and has served on the executive committee of the Commission of Professors of Adult Education (CPAE). In addition to receiving numerous academic and professional awards in the field of adult learning, her co-edited book about distance education, *Harnessing Innovations Technologies in Higher Education,* received the Frandson Book Award from the University Continuing Education Association in 2007, and she received the Lawrence Levin Award from the New York Adult, Community and Continuing Association in 2006.

Human Performance Models Revealed in the Global Context, pages 153–154
Copyright © 2009 by Information Age Publishing

Victor C. X. Wang, EdD, is assistant professor/credential director of vocational and adult education at California State University, Long Beach. Wang's research and writing activities have focused on human performance, the foundations of adult education, adult teaching and learning, training, transformative learning, cultural issues in vocational and adult education, distance education and curriculum development. He has published more than ten books and dozens of chapters and refereed journal articles and has been a reviewer for four journals. He has won many academic achievement awards from different universities in China and in the United States. He taught extensively as a full professor in China in places such as universities, Radio stations and China Central TV (CCTV) prior to coming to study and work in the United States in 1997. He has taught adult learners ESL, Chinese, Computer Technology, Vocational and Adult Education courses, Research Methods, Curriculum Development and Performance Improvement Technology for the past 19 years at university settings. In addition, he has served as a translator/narrator for national and international leaders both in China and in the United States. The videotapes and DVDs he published for national and international leaders are played all over the world both for educational purposes and investment purposes. He co-edited two books (Comparative Adult Education Around The Globe; Innovations in Career and Technical Education: Strategic Approaches Towards Workforce Competencies Around The Globe) with Fordham University Professor, Kathleen P. King, which have been adopted as required textbooks by premium universities in the United States and in China.

ABOUT THE CONTRIBUTORS

Claretha H. Banks is assistant professor who holds a PhD in Career and Technical Education from Virginia Tech. She teaches Human Resource Development and Adult Education courses at University of Arkansas, Fayetteville. Her research interests also focus on the Vocational and Adult Education/Human Resource Development (HRD) area. She holds graduate faculty status and advises graduate students with an interest in Vocational and Adult Education and Human Resource Development. She has extensive professional experience in business and industry and continues to serve as a consultant to international, national, and state organizations.

Jules K. Beck is Assistant Professor at the University of Arkansas. A native of Minneapolis, Minnesota, Beck Attended the University of Chicago and graduated from the University of Minnesota with an MSW and PhD with concentration in Human Resource Development. Beck is a Licensed Certified Social Worker (LCSW) in Arkansas and holds Social Worker Emeritus status in Minnesota. Beck has over three years experience in international community and leadership development in South and Central America, West Africa, and Eastern Europe. He was a two-year volunteer in the community development Project Awareness on White Earth Reservation, Minnesota. Beck taught grades 4–6 in Potosí, Bolivia and high school classes in South Shore, S. Dak. He was a community organizer for 10 years on the Northside of Minneapolis. Beck chaired the St. Louis Park, MN Human Rights Commission and was elected to three terms as president of the ACLU of Minnesota. Beck co-developed a disaster recovery planning system in Spanish as an information technology consultant for a USA accounting firm. Beck is in his tenth year teaching university classes and research in

Human Performance Models Revealed in the Global Context, pages 155–158
155

adult education, human resource development, and business and industry education.

John A. Henschke is Associate Professor and Leader of the Award Winning Adult Education MEd, EdD, and PhD, Program at the University of Missouri, St. Louis, and Continuing Education Specialist with University of Missouri Extension. He is Visiting Professor at the Beijing [PRC] Radio and Television University. He was President of the American Association for Adult and Continuing Education (AAACE), was Chair of the Commission on International Adult Education (CIAE) of AAACE, and is a Member of the Commission of Professors of Adult Education (CPAE). John is a Board Member of the International Adult and Continuing Education Hall of Fame (IAEHOF). He has been involved with testing his ideas in the Field of Adult and Continuing Education (ACE) around the world since 1970.

Nura M. Huka is a Master of Degree holder in Finance and Accounting from University of Nairobi: Bachelor of Commerce, Finance option from University of Nairobi and Qualified Accountant (CPA-K): He has proven experience and skills in facilitating learning processes in a multi cultural setting and various institutions in and outside Kenya. His areas of expertise includes: leadership and management, public sector reforms, financial management among others. He has extensively covered a wider management and administration area; He has a full understanding of the training needs assessment, curriculum and material development. He has participated in various national and international forum and presented papers. Mr. Nura joined the Kenya Institute of Administration in 2004 as a lecturer and rose along the ladder and currently holds a position of Learning and Development Manager. His dream and desire is to see Institute achieve its vision of becoming a model Institution of Excellence in Learning and Development programs delivery.

Margaret Kobia, has a PhD in Education: Human Resource Education from the University of Illinois, Urbana Champaign, 2003, a MEd in Teacher Education, from Kenyatta University in 1991.She is an accomplished management training consultant and an established university faculty member with extensive knowledge in lecturing and research in General Management, Leadership and Entrepreneurship. She has authored and co-authored several refereed research papers. She joined the Kenya Institute of Administration (KIA) in 2005 as Director and Chief Executive. The mandate of the Institute is to promote professionalism and best management practices in the public service. She is ardently committed to enhancing the scope of activities in the institute in the delivery of quality training, research and consultancy services towards public service reform endeavors. She is dedicated to KIA building capacity through partnerships to ensure the delivery of services beyond the customer's expectations.

Fredrick M. Nafukho is Associate Professor of Human Resource Development and Chair, HRD Program of the Department of Educational Administration and Human Resource Development, College of Education and Human Development, Texas A & M, University. He holds a PhD in Human Resource Development, Louisiana State University, where he was a Fulbright Scholar, and MEd (Economics of Education), and BEd Business Education and Economics from Kenyatta University, Kenya. In his 16 years of experience working in higher education, he has also served as Associate Professor and Assistant Department Head, University of Arkansas, Fayetteville, Head, Department of Educational Administration and Curriculum Development, Moi University Kenya. Nafukho has published over 120 articles, chapters, and books. His primary area of research has been aligned with investment in human capital, enrollment modeling and prediction in higher education, E-learning, and performance improvement. He served as Proceedings Editor and Chair of the Academy of Human Resource Development Annual Conferences, 2006–2007. He is board member of the AHRD Executive Board, and serves as Editorial Board Member of *Human Resource Development Quarterly, Advances in Developing Human Resources, Journal of Eastern Africa Research and Development.* He teaches courses in Adult Education and Human Resource Development.

Ramesh Sharma holds a PhD in Education in the area of Educational Technology and is currently working as Regional Director in Indira Gandhi National Open University (IGNOU). He has been a teacher trainer and has taught Educational Technology, Educational Research and Statistics, Educational Measurement and Evaluation, Special Education, Psychodynamics of Mental Health Courses. He has conducted many Human Development training programs for the in- and pre-service teachers. He had established a Center of ICT in the College he was working. He is a member of many committees on implementation of technology in the Open University. His areas of specialization include staff development, on-line learning, student support services in open and distance learning, and teacher education. He is a member of Advisory Group meeting on Human Resources Development for the *United Nations Conference on Trade and Development* (UNCTAD). He is the co-Editor of *Asian Journal of Distance Education* (www.ASIANJDE.org). In addition to these, he is/has been on the Editorial Advisory Board of numerous journals related to distance learning including, *International Review of Research in Open and Distance Learning, Turkish Online Journal of Distance Education and Distance Education.* He has co-authored and co-edited books on distance education research, including *Interactive Multimedia in Education and Training* and *Cases on Global E-Learning Practices: Successes and Pitfalls.*

Gabriele Strohschen, EdD, is assistant professor and faculty mentor at DePaul University's School for New Learning (SNL). As former Director for the Graduate Programs of SNL she designed and implemented the school's first transnational graduate program in Thailand and its first MA in facilitating adult learning. She mentors and teaches in SNL's student-designed programs. Most recently, she has worked as Visiting Professor and Dissertation Advisor at Assumption University (Bangkok, Thailand) and Burapha University (Bangsaen, Thailand). She was the inaugural director of National-Louis University's online graduate program in adult and continuing education from 1997 to 2003. She conducts professional development seminars for adult educators in North America, Europe, Latin America, and Southeast Asia. After two decades of working in community organizing in Chicago's inner-city communities, she entered academia and now also provides program design and staff training for refugee and immigrant NGOs and public education institutions as a volunteer consultant in Chicago.

INDEX

A

AAPKC (Asociación Afro-Paraguaya
    Kamba Cua), 119–120
Adenauer, Konrad, 47
Adult education. *See* Andragogy
African study/performance contracting
    and practices, 81–82, 100–101
    countries using performance
        contracting in public sector,
        84, 85, 86–87
    lessons learned, 87
    employment meaning in some
        African countries, 84
    performance contracting
        definitions, 83
    rationales for contracts, 84–85
    research directions (future), 100
    See also Gambia; Ghana; Kenya;
        Swaziland
American Society for Training and
    Development (ASTD)
    competencies related to human
        performance improvement, 67
    Models for Human Performance
        Improvement, 69

Andragogy, 10
    conceptual framework assumptions,
        10–12
    the learner, 10
    learning motivation, 11
    learning orientation, 11
    readiness to learn, 11
    reasons for learning, 11–12
    role of learner's experience, 10–11
    vs. pedagogy, 12
Argentina
    /Bolivia grassroots development,
        116–117
    market reforms, 108–109
Asia-Pacific Programme of Educational
    Innovation for Development
    (APEID)/UNESCO, 57–58
Asociación de Recicladores Las Marías,
    118–119

B

Bolivia
    grassroots development, 116–117
    market reform, 109
    political alliances, 112

Human Performance Models Revealed in the Global Context, pages 159–165
Copyright © 2009 by Information Age Publishing

Printed in the United States
130152LV00001BB/10-27/P

9 781607 520115